MATRICULATION HISTORY OF ENGLAND

MATRICULATION HISTORY OF ENGLAND

H L O GARRETT

GYAN

Published by

Gyan Publishing House
5, Ansari Road
Daryaganj, New Delhi-110002
Phone: 011-47034999, 9811692060
E-mail: books@gyanbooks.com

Distribution Network
gyanbooks.com
India, USA, Canada, UK, Australia

ISBN: 978-93-7447-311-5 (PB)

First Published, 1930

2nd Impression 2026

Printed at: Gyan Press, Delhi.

MATRICULATION HISTORY OF ENGLAND
Author: H L O GARRETT

Matriculation History of England

FOR INDIAN HIGH SCHOOLS

BY

H. L. O. GARRETT, M.A., I.E.S.,
Principal, Government College, Lahore.

LAHORE
UTTAR CHAND KAPUR & SONS
1930

PREFATORY NOTE.

'History and Geography' was an elective subject under the old regulations for the Matriculation and School Leaving Certificate Examination and candidates could offer only two out of the four papers on General Geography, Commercial Geography, History of India and History of England. The result was that the number of boys taking the subject showed a rapid decrease and a very large majority of those who left school betrayed a lamentable ignorance of the simplest facts of English History; in fact, it was found that they were ill-equipped for study at College. To remedy this state of affairs, the curriculum for the M. and S. L. C. Examination was thoroughly revised. Under the new regulations which come into force from the examination of 1929, History and Geography is not only a compulsory subject but also includes the History of India, the History of England, and General Geography. As a consequence of these modifications, the syllabus in English History has undergone most important changes and rightly lays emphasis on the later period.

My excuse for writing this book is that I am not aware of any that would meet the requirements of Punjab schoolboys reading for the M. and S. L. C. Examination. The book is an attempt to satisfy a pressing need and I have, therefore, carefully followed the new syllabus laid down by the University. I agree with the view that, as regards the earlier portion of English History, a bare outline is sufficient for the schoolboys at this stage. Hence I have confined myself in this part to a very simple narration of essential facts such as the Norman

Conquest, Magna Charta, the Reformation, etc., omitting all unnecessary details.

From 1603 the story is told in much greater detail, for it is from this point that the expansion of England as a World Power really commences and it is from this point that a knowledge of English History becomes of more value to the Indian schoolboy. It will be noticed that the language employed is easy, simple and intelligible: nothing takes away from the interest of the subject so much as difficulty of language.

I am greatly indebted to Bakhshi Ram Rattan for his valuable assistance in compiling the book—particularly the later chapters—and shall welcome suggestions for improvement from teachers in the light of their experience.

LAHORE,
September, 1927.

H. L. O. G.

SECOND EDITION.

In the new edition, certain additions have been made as the outcome of suggestions from teachers.

LAHORE,
January, 1930.

H. L. O. G.

CHAPTER I

CHAPTER II

CHAPTER III

CHAPTER IV

CHAPTER V

CHAPTER VI

CHAPTER VII

CHAPTER VIII

CHAPTER IX

CHAPTER X

CHAPTER XI

CHAPTER XII

CHAPTER XIII

CHAPTER XIV

CHAPTER XV

CHAPTER XVI

CHAPTER XVII

CHAPTER XVIII

LIST OF ILLUSTRATIONS

CHAPTER I.

England before the Norman Conquest.

In reading the history of the various countries in the world we find that, in most cases, there have been a number of invasions. The invaders have, in their turn, been conquered by fresh invaders, till finally the modern nation is built up as we find it to-day. Here in India we read of invasions of Aryans, Rajputs, Afghans, Mughals, etc. And so it is in the history of England. Britain, to give it the name by which it was known in earlier days, was first inhabited by a people called the Iberians. We do not know much about these people. What we do know is mostly derived from remains that have been dug up—weapons, pottery, etc.—just as to-day in India such remains of early people are being found.

The Britons.

Many many years ago the Iberians were conquered by a people called the Britons. The Britons were of the Celtic race—of the same family as the Gauls who then inhabited France. They were a much more civilized people than the Iberians and were divided into a number of tribes. We know much more about the Britons than about the Iberians because they came into contact with the Romans, who were then the most powerful nation in Europe. The

Romans had conquered the Gauls who lived in what is now France, and the Britons had helped the latter, so the Romans made up their minds to cross the English Channel and punish the Britons. The Romans were commanded by the famous General Julius Cæsar. Cæsar defeated the Britons in battle, though he did not conquer the island. He was an author as well as a soldier and he wrote an account of the Britons which tells us a good deal about them. Some years after Cæsar's death, which took place in 44 B.C., Britain was gradually conquered by the Romans and became a province of their Empire. The Romans never conquered Scotland but built a stone wall across the north of Britain to keep out the Scots, the remains of which can still be seen to-day.

Roman Britain.

Under Roman rule the Britons were happy and contented. They adopted many Roman customs and many of them lived in the Roman style. The Romans remained in Britain for nearly 400 years. At last trouble in Italy forced them to take away the last of their troops, in 410 A.D. The Britons were left helpless, for they had forgotten how to fight and had been content to let the Romans protect them.

The Anglo-Saxons.

A helpless people is always at the mercy of those who are stronger and the Britons soon found enemies on all sides. The Scots in the north broke down the wall and invaded the country. And other enemies came from oversea. From what is now Denmark came a number of tribes, Angles, Saxons, Jutes,

etc. who gradually overran the whole country and drove the remains of the Britons into the extreme west and into the mountains of Wales. Under the Romans, the Britons had become Christians. But the new invaders were heathen and they destroyed the churches and put the priests to death. They were an agricultural people and hated town life. Hence they destroyed most of the towns that the Romans had built. This explains why so few Roman remains are to be found in Britain to-day.

The new invaders soon divided up the country between them and from one of them—the Angles—it got its new name of Angle-land or England. After a time the country became divided up into seven distinct kingdoms.

Sometimes one kingdom and sometimes another became stronger than the others and was acknowledged as head. In the end the Kings of the Western Kingdom, called Wessex, became more powerful than all the rest, and Kings of all England. Our present King to-day is descended from this family of Saxon Kings.

As the Anglo-Saxons settled down in England they gradually became civilized and gave up their old fierce habits. Missionaries from Rome converted them to Christianity and churches once more sprang up all over the land.

Some of the Saxon Kings were learned and clever men. The most famous of them was Alfred the Great.

Alfred was not only a great scholar. He was a good soldier and is often called the "Father of the British Navy" because he saw that the best protection of England against her enemies was a strong fleet. He therefore had one made. And this fleet was needed because, in the reign of Alfred, new enemies invaded the country. These were called Northmen or Danes. They were brave and hardy sailors and they attacked many other parts of Europe as well. They crossed the sea in their swift ships and seized a large part of the east and centre of England. King Alfred was at first defeated by them and almost driven from his throne. But in the end he defeated them and their leader agreed to make peace and to become a Christian. He and his followers were given a part of the country to live in and they soon settled down as peaceful citizens. After the death of Alfred (901 A.D.) his descendants reigned over England for nearly 200 years but they were often troubled by fresh invasions of Danes and for a time were driven out altogether and a Dane—Canute—became King of England.

Alfred the Great.

Although he was a Dane, Canute proved a very good King and kept order in the country. He was a wise man and a story is told of him which shows this. One day his courtiers were pattering him and telling him that he was such a great King that everything in the world would obey him. The King ordered his chair to be placed at the edge of the sea. After a time the tide began to flow up and the water

King Canute.

ENGLAND
on the eve of the
NORMAN CONQUEST
Scale 1 6,000,000 (100 miles 1 inch)
English Miles
0
50
100
SUDREYS
SCOTLAND
LOTHIAN
Edinburgh
Clyde
Carham
Tweed
Holy I
Bamburgh
BERNICIA
NORTHUMBRIA
Tyne
Jarrow
Chester le Streete
Durham
CUMBRIA
Eden
WESTMORLAND
Tees
Swale
Ure
Wharfe
Man
(Morcar)
Stamford Br
Fulford
Riccall
York
Tadcaster
Ribble
Aire
Don
Ouse
IRISH SEA
NORTH
SEA
Humber
Manchester
Mersey
Gainsborough
Lincoln
Trent
Anglesey
Chester
The Wash
Dee
MERCIA
(Edwin)
Stafford
Derby
Nottingham
Stamford
Leicester
Shrewsbury
Severn
Coventry
Warwick
Worcester
Nen
Ouse
Ely
Norwich
EAST
ANGLIA
Thetford
Northampton
Huntingdon
Waltheof
Leominster
Wye
Hereford
Teifi
Towy
Usk
Avon
Gloucester
Bedford
Ipswich
Ringmere
(Gyrth)
Hertford
Maldon
Waltham
Oxford
Wallingford
Fyfield
Sherston
London
Brentford
Thames
Thanet
Sandwich
Canterbury
Dover
Bristol
Avon
Wells
Watchet
Glastonbury
Penselwood
Winchester
Otford
(Leofwine)
WESSEX
(Harold)
Parret
Southampton
Bosham
Battle
Hastings
Pevensey
Exe
Exeter
Tamar
Wight
ENGLISH CHANNEL
A
4
B
West from 2 Greenwich
C
0
D

came to the King's chair. "Sea," said the King, "come no further." Of course the tide continued to flow and soon the King's legs were wet. "See how foolishly you talk," said the King. "You tell me that everything in the world will obey me, yet I cannot even control the sea." The foolish courtiers were silent.

Edward the Confessor.

After his death troubles arose and his sons quarrelled among themselves. In 1042, the Saxon Kings came back in the person of Edward, the last real Saxon King of England. Edward was a bad King as he was weak and could not keep order. But he was a very pious man and got the name of Edward the Confessor. He is famous as the builder of Westminster Abbey, though very little of his building can be seen to-day.

The Normans.

Before he became King, Edward had spent many years in exile in Normandy. Normandy is a district in the north of France which had been occupied by another band of Northmen, of the same race as the Danes who had invaded England. The Northmen, or Normans as they were called in France, settled in Normandy and gave their name to the country. Edward was very friendly with William, the Duke of Normandy. Indeed he made him a promise that, when he died, William should succeed him as King of England. When Edward became King he brought many Normans into England and gave them offices there. When Edward died in 1066 the Saxon nobles, instead of inviting William to be king, chose one of their own number Harold, a brave man and a good soldier. William was very angry when he heard this and made up his mind to lead an army over to England and get the crown by force. He promised to give to all who would come with him lands and positions in England, so he soon collected a large army.

Norman Conquest.

In October 1066 he landed at Pevensey on the south coast of England. Harold hurried to meet him and the two armies met at Senlac. For a long time the Saxons stood firm and the Normans could not defeat them. At last Harold was fatally wounded by an arrow which struck him in the eye and the Saxons were soon hopelessly beaten. William then advanced to London where he forced the leading men to elect him as their King and, on Christmas Day 1066, he was crowned in Westminster Abbey. To the Saxons the victory of William seemed an evil thing. But the Norman Conquest was really a very good thing for England. The Saxons were a rough, backward people and England was far behind the rest of Europe in civilization. The Normans, who were a very clever and highly civilized people, introduced many changes into the country which made England no longer a backward little island but one of the leading nations of Europe.

THE BATTLE OF HASTINGS

CHAPTER II.

England under the Normans.

William I 1066—1087.

William had not much difficulty in subduing England. There was some trouble in the north and in the marshes of the east a brave Saxon, called Hereward the Wake, held out for a time. But William soon crushed these risings. Most of the old Saxon landlords were turned out—indeed a great many of them had fallen at Hastings with their King—and William put Normans in their place. In doing this he introduced what is called the Feudal System. By this system every one held his land from someone else and was bound to produce armed men if required and to render other services.

The Feudal System.

A man who held land from another was called a tenant or a vassal. Those who held their land direct from the King were called tenants-in-chief. When one man received a grant of land from another he went through a solemn ceremony called 'Homage.' Unarmed and bareheaded he knelt before his lord and took a solemn oath that he would be faithful to him and perform all the services which were due. Each piece of land was assessed for the purpose of what was called military service, that is to say, the owner had to give so many armed men to serve for 40 days if required. Besides this the tenant had to fix presents on certain occasions, very much in the same way as we see *nazrs* here in India presented in darbars. If his lord's daughter got married, for example, he had to make a present. Apart from the free landowners there was a great number of people who were not free and who were called villeins. This word really means 'native,' that is one born on the land. The villein was not unlike our *kamin* in the Punjab. He was not a slave for he could not be bought and sold. But he was not free and was not allowed to leave the service of the man upon whose land he had been born. He was obliged to work for his lord and in return he got his share of the produce of the estate to keep him and his family. If he would not work his master could punish him but could not put him to death, as this could only be done by the King's court.

There were villeins in most countries of Europe but, after the great rebellion in the reign of Richard II, the English villeins won their freedom, while those in other countries, like France and Russia, had to wait many years before they became free.

The danger of the feudal system was that a great feudal lord might become so powerful that he might refuse to obey the king. William himself had been a feudal lord in Normandy—as Duke of Normandy he held his land from the King of France—and he knew the danger of the system.

He made up his mind to prevent this from happening in England and he did this in two ways. He was careful not to give one man all his land in one place, so that he might not become too powerful Secondly he called together a great meeting of the feudal landowners and made them swear that they would obey the king first and not their own lord. By such means he kept order and it was only when later kings were too weak to make the landowners obey them that trouble occurred.

Doomsday Book.

William was anxious to find out how much his new kingdom was worth and how much revenue he might expect to get from it. So he sent men all over the country to make a list of lands, cattle, and houses. Men complained that not even a single pig was left out. All this information was put into a great book called the Doomsday Book. Doom means judgment and it was so called because a decision could be made by referring to the book. This reminds us very much of the summary settlement of the Punjab made in 1849, when the British, like William, were anxious to find out what the value of the Punjab was and how much revenue they were likely to get from it.

The New Forest.

William was very fond of hunting and to provide himself with a good place for this he turned a part of the South of England into a forest. This forest still exists and, though it is now over 800 years old, it is still called the New Forest.

Hard and stern though he was, William ruled England well and justly. It was said that in his time a man might travel from one end of England to the other with a bag full of gold and that no one would dare to rob him. After a reign of 21 years he died in 1087, as the result of an accident while riding.

William II 1087—1100.

His eldest son Robert became Duke of Normandy and his second son William succeeded him as King of England. William II was called Rufus—the Red—from the colour of his hair and he proved a thoroughly bad king. He was very wicked and he quarrelled with everybody. He made war upon his brother Robert and he seized the property of the Church and ill-treated the bishops. In 1100 his reign came suddenly to an end. He had gone out hunting in the New Forest and then came the news that the Red King had been found lying dead with an arrow through his heart. To this day no one knows whether he was murdered or whether he had met with an accident. But no one was sorry for such a wicked man.

Henry I 1100—1135.

His younger brother Henry now came to the throne as Henry I. He was a different man to his brother in every way. He was a good ruler and men called him the Lion of Justice. He took an English princess as his wife and did his best to make the English like him. In Normandy he made war upon his brother Robert and took away that country from him. Robert was taken prisoner and Henry shut him up in a castle for the rest of his life.

Henry had only one son—William—and in 1120 a great sorrow fell upon the King. Prince William and some of his friends were crossing over for Normandy to England in a ship called the 'White Ship.' They were all very merry and had given the sailors too much wine to drink. The result was that the ship was carelessly run upon a rock and all on board except one man were drowned. The Prince got into a small boat and might have escaped but he turned back to save a lady who had been left on the ship, and his boat was sunk by others jumping into it. It is said that after the King heard the news he never smiled again.

Henry had now only a daughter left. This lady's name was Maud and she had been married twice, first to the Holy Roman Emperor, who ruled at Vienna. But the Emperor died and she married a French noble, the Count of Anjou.

Henry now persuaded all the great men to promise that when he died they would recognize Maud as queen.

Not long after this Henry died, in 1135, after a reign of 35 years.

Stephen 1135—1154.

No sooner was he dead than many of the great men forgot their promise and, making the excuse that they could not be ruled by a woman, chose her cousin Stephen as king. Stephen was a weak, easygoing man, and the great lords thought that if he were king they could do as they liked. But Maud soon landed in England and a civil war began between Stephen and herself. It was a miserable time. The great lords did not care much who won the war. But it gave them an opportunity to do what they liked and they committed all sorts of cruel deeds. Plundering and looting went on unchecked and men were seized and tortured for the sake of their wealth. At last after 18 years of civil war a peace was made and it was arranged that Stephen should be king for the rest of his life and that on his death he should be succeeded by Henry who was the son of Maud by her second husband, the Count of Anjou.

Stephen died soon after this, in 1154, and Henry became King as Henry II. Stephen was the last of the Norman Kings. With Henry II begins a new line of kings who are sometimes called Anjevins—because they came from Anjou—and sometimes Plantagenets. This word means the broom flower, which was the badge of the family.

The reign of Stephen shows the worst side of the feudal system, the great lords being free to do exactly what they liked while the King was too weak or too busy with the civil war to force them to behave properly.

CHAPTER III

The Early Plantagenet Kings.

Henry II 1154—1189.

When Henry II became King of England in 1154, he found himself the ruler of a very large kingdom. Not only was he King of England, but he was ruler of a great part of France, more even than the King of France himself possessed. From his father he inherited the lands of Anjou and he took as his wife a French princess who owned broad lands in the south of France.

During most of his reign Henry was on bad terms with the King of France and was often at war with him as the French King was jealous of him and wanted to take away his lands in France.

Henry proved a very great King indeed—one of the greatest who have ever ruled in England.

Henry restores order.

His first duty was to restore order, for the country was in a sad state of confusion after the troubles of Stephen's reign. Henry put down disorder with a strong hand. He pulled down many castles which had been built without permission. Also he made men obey the law. In those days many people in England held law courts of their own. Henry tried to stop this. He sent out his judges on tour all over England to hold courts and to enforce one system of law which should be common to the whole country. This system has been continued from his time to the present day. Henry also provided for the proper defence of the country and made all men train themselves in the use of arms. He was always busy working hard to improve the state of the country. It is said that he never slept two nights running in the same place.

Henry and the Church.

Henry's reforms led him into one great quarrel. This was with the Church. The Church at that time claimed the right to try all clergy in its own courts. In those days the clergy meant practically everyone who could read or write. Anyone who could prove that he could do so was given what was called "benefit of clergy" and could only be tried in the church courts.

Many clergy were bad men who committed many serious crimes. But they could only be tried in the church courts and these courts were not able to give really severe punishments. They could only turn the offender out of the Church and a really bad man would not care much for that.

Thomas Becket.

Henry wanted to stop this and so he got his friend, Thomas Becket, made Archbishop of Canterbury. Becket was the son of a rich London merchant and he and the King had been friends for years. Henry had made him Lord Chancellor and in those days the Lord Chancellor was the principal minister and adviser of the King. Becket did not want to become Archbishop at all, for he knew

that if he did so he would be obliged to maintain the rights of the Church and would no longer be friendly with the King. But the King hoped that if Becket became Archbishop he would help him in reforming the Church. So when Becket became Archbishop he would not do as the King wished. They were both hot-tempered men and a violent quarrel broke out between them. In the end the King flew into a temper and cried out 'Will no one rid me of this priest?' Four of his followers heard these words and thought they would earn Henry's favour by killing Becket. They hurried to Canterbury and murdered Becket in his own cathedral in 1170.

The murder of Becket caused great horror all over Europe. Henry was obliged to humble himself publicly before the grave of Becket and to give up all idea of interfering with the power of the Church.

Becket was looked upon as a martyr and his tomb became a famous place where pilgrims from all over Europe came to visit.

Death of Henry II.

The last part of Henry's reign was mainly spent in France. Henry's sons rebelled against him and took the side of the King of France. This was a great shock to the old King and, when he learnt that his youngest and favourite son John had also turned against him, he took to his bed and soon died in great grief in 1189. It was a sad end for such a great King.

He was succeeded by his son Richard I who was a very brave soldier and was called the Lion Heart. Richard was hardly an English King at all. Most of his reign was spent in Palestine fighting to recover the Holy Land from the Saracens. Christian pilgrims had visited Palestine for many years to pray at the Holy Places of the Christian religion. The early Mohammedan conquerors of Palestine had not interfered with these pilgrims. But now the Saracens began to ill treat them, so the Christian nations sent armies to Palestine to reconquer the land and make it safe for the pilgrims. Between the years 1095 and 1270 there was a number of these wars in Palestine which were known as the Crusades, or wars of the cross. There were seven Crusades altogether and they were a failure, as the Christian powers of Europe never succeeded in getting back the Holy Land. The Crusade in which King Richard took part was the third of these expeditions. In 1199 Richard was killed while besieging a castle in France and his younger brother John became King.

Richard I 1189—1199.

There are few people in history about whom we can say nothing good. John was one of them. He was cruel, treacherous, and wicked. He was hated in England for no one could trust him. He also quarrelled with the Pope who tried to turn him off his throne.

John 1199—1216.

He made war on the King of France but he was so unsuccessful that he lost most of the lands

KING JOHN SEALS THE MAGNA CHARTA

his father had possessed.

When he was beaten in France he came back to England. But he had no soldiers left and the great men made up their minds that they would now force him to govern properly.

The Great Charter.

And so a great meeting was held at Runnymede on the Thames in 1215. At this meeting a paper was drawn up and given to King John and he was obliged to agree to it. This paper was called the Great Charter. It is a very important paper because it prevented the King from governing badly and protected the liberty of the people. Hence it is sometimes called the foundation stone of British liberty. In this Charter the King was made to promise that he would not take money from his subjects without their consent. He had also to declare that he would administer justice fairly and speedily and that he would not imprison any free man, except after proper trial. The Kings who came after John were obliged to renew the Charter and promise to keep it. Altogether it was renewed thirty-two times.

John died in the next year—1216. He left things in a great state of confusion. The heir to the throne was his son Henry who was only a boy. A French army had invaded England to carry out the order of the Pope and turn John out.

However the French were persuaded to go away and one of the greatest of the English nobles, the Earl of Pembroke, became the guardian of the boy-King and ruled wisely and well.

Henry III 1216—1272.

When Henry III grew up he proved a very bad King. He was weak and was very much in the hands of his wife's relations, to whom he gave lands and money. This made the English nobles angry, for the King gave away so much that he was always in debt and could not govern properly. Again and again he broke the conditions of the Great Charter although he had promised to keep them. Things grew so bad that the nobles joined together and drew up a paper called the Provisions of Oxford, because it was prepared at that city, by which they took the government out of the King's hands altogether and put it into the control of a committee of themselves. But even this did not stop the misgovernment.

The Barons' War.

At last the nobles led by the King's brother-in-law, Simon de Montfort, Earl of Leicester, took the power out of the King's hands altogether. Then a civil war broke out between the King and the nobles. A battle was fought at Lewes in 1265 in which the King was defeated and he and his son Edward were taken prisoners.

The First Parliament.

Simon de Montfort now became ruler of England for a short time and he did his best to govern well. In 1265 he called together the first English Parliament. Up to this time England had been ruled

WESTMINSTER ABBEY

by the King and his Council. But now Simon called together men elected by the counties and the towns to take counsel about the affairs of the country.

Simon's rule did not last long. The other nobles grew jealous of him and Prince Edward escaped from prison and joined them.

Simon and his sons were caught by their enemies at Evesham in 1267 and in the battle he and his sons were killed. He was a great man and his work lived after him, for when Parliament began to meet regularly some years later, it was called together in the way first started by Simon de Montfort. Hence he is sometimes called the Founder of the English Parliament.

Henry III reigned in peace for five years after the death of Simon de Montfort and died in 1272.

Westminster Abbey.

Apart from the troubles with the nobles and the meeting of the first Parliament his reign is chiefly famous for the building of Westminster Abbey, the famous church in London in which all the Kings and Queens since William I have been crowned. Henry III pulled down the older church built by Edward the Confessor and built a new and more beautiful church, most of which is to be seen to-day. Henry was a very religious man and he spent a very large sum of money in building the Abbey. Indeed one of the main complaints against him was that he was always short of money and always asking for more because he spent so much on the building of the Abbey.

CHAPTER IV

The Later Plantagenets.

Edward I 1272—1307.

By the end of the reign of Henry III the Saxons and the Normans had become one people—the English. The loss of the lands in France had much to do with this. Most of the great lords had land in both countries and divided their time between the two. But now that many of them had lost their lands in France they settled down in England altogether and so the two people began to draw together. A new language came to be the language of the country—the English language,—which was a mixture of Anglo-Saxon and Norman-French.

The new King, Edward I, was a very great King indeed. He was a great soldier, a great administrator, and a great lawgiver.

Edward's laws.

Let us take his laws first. At the very beginning of his reign he made a number of laws which are of very great importance even today. All our system of the ownership of property and of inheritance in England depended upon them for many years. As a result of the laws passed by him much of the property in England came to be held in what is called entail. This meant that the owner for the time being is only the owner for life. He cannot sell or divide up the property. He can make what he can out of it during his lifetime and any such money is called his personal property and he can do what he likes with it. But the estate is what is called real property and, on the death of the owner, it passes, as a matter of course, to the next heir. From his reign also begin the regular courts of law where only one form of justice was given—that of the King. As we have seen, before King Edward's time, there were many different kinds of law courts and different kinds of law all over England. King Edward very largely put a stop to this and so one form of law grew up which was called the Common Law of England because it was common to the whole country.

Conquest of Wales.

Now as to King Edward as a soldier. For many years the English had much trouble with the Welsh. The Welsh who were the descendants of the ancient Britons, were a hardy race of mountaineers and it had been found very difficult to conquer them.

King Edward made up his mind to conquer the Welsh once and for all. So he led an army into Wales. Llewellyn, the last independent Prince of Wales, was killed in battle and Edward became master of the whole country. But the Welsh complained that they had no longer any prince. Just at this time King Edward's wife, who had come with him to Wales, gave birth to their eldest son. Edward brought out the baby and showed it to the Welsh chiefs and said: 'Here is your Prince.' And ever since that day the eldest sons of the Kings of England have borne the title of 'Prince of Wales.'

Edward and the Scots.

From Wales Edward turned to Scotland. Here a dispute had arisen as to who should be king. In 1286, Alexander III the last King of Scotland had fallen down a high cliff while riding in the dark and had been killed. He left only one child behind him—a daughter, Margaret, who was called the Maid of Norway because she had been brought up in that country. Edward now proposed to unite the two countries by arranging a marriage between his young son and the Maid of Norway. The Scots agreed to this but before the marriage could take place the Maid of Norway died. A number of relations now claimed the throne and the Scots decided to refer the matter to Edward and ask him to act as an umpire. Edward said he would do this but first he asked the Scots if the king whom he should choose would acknowledge him as his superior. In the old days the Kings of Scotland had done this but in the time of King Richard I the claim had been given up in return for a sum of money which was badly needed by Richard to pay for his expenses in the Crusades. The Scots now agreed to go back to the old state of things. Edward then called a council at Norham in 1292 to examine the various claims to the throne. Two men had much stronger claims than the

others. These were John Balliol and Robert Bruce. Edward finally decided in favour of John Balliol, who recognized Edward as his overlord and was then crowned King of Scotland.

Conquest of Scotland.

But the Scots soon found that King Edward really regarded himself as the ruler of Scotland, for he began to interfere in their affairs. One thing that he did was to order that appeals should go from the Scottish courts to his own courts in London. This meant a long and sometimes dangerous journey in those days when the roads were very bad and there were many robbers about. This made the Scots very angry and they broke into rebellion. King Edward then marched into Scotland with an army and conquered the whole country. As a sign of this victory he took away the famous stone of Scotland. Upon this stone all the Kings of Scotland had been crowned up to this time. King Edward brought the stone to England and put it in Westminster Abbey, having a chair made of which it formed the seat. Since then it has been used for the coronation of every king or queen of England. There was an old saying about this stone that wherever it went Scottish Kings would reign. This saying came true in 1603 when James VI of Scotland became James I of England and was crowned king upon this stone. The Scots broke into rebellion twice after this in King Edward's reign, first under a brave soldier called William Wallace, whom the Scots still regard as their great national hero.

Secondly under Robert Bruce, and King Edward was on the march against the latter when he died in 1307.

All these wars cost money and Edward's difficulties were made greater by the fact that France also made war on England and sent help to the Scots.

The Model Parliament.

As the danger threatened everybody the King felt that he should call the whole nation to consult with him. And so in 1295 he called together the famous Model Parliament. Like the Parliament of Simon de Montfort of 1265 it was made up of representatives of the Church, the Lords, and the Commons. In the House of Lords sat the Bishops and the Lords. In the House of Commons sat the representatives of the counties and of the towns. This Model Parliament is sometimes called the "Mother of Parliaments" for all other Parliaments have been copied from it. Since 1295 England has always had a Parliament. Sometimes it has not met for some years, but the Kings have always found it necessary to call Parliament together to get money for governing the country and to make laws.

Edward II 1307—1327.

Great men often have bad sons and so it was in the case of Edward I. His son who came to the throne as Edward II was no good at all. He was lazy and idle and was always in the hands of bad favourites. His father had left orders that the war with Scotland was to be carried on after his death. But his son took no notice of this and so the Scots gradually drove the English out of all Scotland except the Castle of Stirling. At last even the lazy King was obliged to do something and he led an army into Scotland to try and save Stirling. But he was a bad General and his army was utterly defeated by Robert Bruce at the battle of Bannockburn in 1314. After this defeat he went back to England and gave up all idea of conquering Scotland. Peace was made for a time between the two countries but they were never friendly and for many years were often at war with one another.

The rest of the reign of Edward the Second was mainly occupied in quarrels with the barons and with his wife, Isabella, who was a French princess. At last the barons made up their mind to turn him out altogether. Parliament met and voted that Edward was not fit to be king any longer. And so he was made to resign and his son took his place as Edward III. He was soon afterwards murdered.

CHAPTER V

The Later Plantagenets (*continued*)

Edward III 1327—1377.

For a time Edward was in the hands of his mother and some of the barons. But he soon freed himself from their control and began to govern for himself. He married a very good wife, Philippa, who came from Flanders and they had a large family of sons.

The 100 Years' War.

Edward III was a great soldier and most of his reign was occupied by a war with France. This war, which broke out in 1338 and lasted till 1453, is known as the Hundred Years' War. This does not mean that the two nations were fighting for a hundred years, but that during that time they were on bad terms with one another and were often at war. The causes of the Hundred Years' War were the following:—

1. The French had helped the Scots against the English.

2. The English and French sailors were constantly fighting in the English Channel.

3. The French interfered with the English Wool Trade with Flanders. In those days the principal source of wealth in England was the rearing of sheep and the exporting of their wool to Flanders to be made into cloth.

4. The position of the English lands in France.

Though nearly all the old possessions were lost the English still held the province of Gascony in the south. The French claimed that the King of England held this land as a dependant of the King of France. The English claimed that Gascony was as much a part of the King's dominions as England itself. And so for these reasons the war broke out in 1338. Soon after this King Edward made another claim. He claimed to be the King of France itself.

The last three Kings of France, who were all brothers, had died leaving no children. Their sister was Isabella, the mother of Edward III. Now in France there was a law called the Salic Law by which no woman could come to the throne.

So Isabella was passed over and her cousin Philip was made king. Edward III, however, claimed that, while his mother could not be queen, she could pass on her right to him and that therefore he, and not Philip, was the rightful King of France.

Progress of the War.

Little happened in the early part of the war except that the English won a great naval victory at Sluys in 1340. But in 1346, Edward determined to invade France and crossed over with a large army. The French met him at Cressy and a battle took place in which King Edward won a great victory. This victory and the many others won by the English in the war were due to the English archers. These men were armed with the long bow—a weapon 8 feet long—and they were so quick and skilful that the French, who usually fought on horseback, were shot down before they could get near them. King Edward took very little part in the battle of Cressy as he wished his eldest son, Edward, to have the chief credit. The French pressed so hard upon the part of the army commanded by the Prince that the officers with him sent to the King for help. "Is my son dead, unhorsed, or so badly wounded that he cannot support himself?" asked the King. "Nothing of the sort," said the messenger, "but he is in so hot an engagement that he is in great need of your help." "Return to those who sent you," said the King, "and tell them from me not to send again for me this day nor expect that I shall come, as long as my son has life: and say that I command them to let the boy win his spurs, for I am determined that all the glory of this day shall be given to him." The Prince was only a boy but he fought bravely and won for himself the title of the Black Prince, from the colour of his armour.

After Cressy King Edward laid siege to Calais—an important town in the north. After a time the garrison were forced to surrender from hunger and for 200 years Calais remained an English town.

Ten years later, in 1356, the Black Prince won another great victory over the French at Poitiers and took their King John prisoner.

At last peace was made in 1360 and the war came to an end for a time.

The Black Prince had worn himself out with all this fighting and he returned to England an invalid. He died, before his father, in 1376.

The Black Death.

During the reign of King Edward a fearful outbreak of the plague visited England. It was called the Black Death and it was worst in 1348 and 1349. Hundreds and thousands of people died of it and labour became difficult to get. Hence the labourers tried to get higher wages, and Parliament tried to stop this in 1351 by passing a law called the Statute of Labourers, which forbade men to demand higher wages. Apart from this the chief business of Parliament in the reign of King Edward was to vote him money for the war.

The later part of his reign was very sad. After his good queen died, King Edward fell into the hands of unworthy favourites. His sons quarrelled among themselves and the old King was too feeble to stop them. At last he died in 1377, deserted by everybody.

Richard II 1377—1399. The Peasants' Revolt.

As the Black Prince was dead, his son came to the throne as King Richard II. He was only a boy of ten at the time and so was largely under the control of his uncles. Soon after his accession a great rebellion broke out in England known as the Peasants' Revolt of 1381. The Statute of Labourers had made the labourers very discontented and now the Government decided to raise a tax upon everyone in the country above a certain age. The labourers then broke into rebellion in the south and east of England under the leadership of a man called Wat Tyler. They marched on London where they did a good deal of damage. The young King showed great courage in dealing with them and Wat Tyler himself was killed for insulting the King. His followers were persuaded to go home by making various promises to them. These promises were not carried out but the labourers had shown their power and enjoyed much more freedom in the future.

Richard's bad government.

When Richard grew up he did not prove a very good king. He had a very bad temper and a king who cannot keep his temper is always in difficulties. At last, in 1387, some of the barons headed by one of his uncles took the power out of his hands. Richard submitted for the time and soon got his power back again. Then he governed very well for a number of years. But he was only waiting for his revenge. In 1397 he suddenly arrested those who had attacked him ten years before; and put some of them to death, including his uncle. The remainder were punished and some of them were sent into exile, among others his cousin, Henry Earl of Derby. Henry's father was John of Gaunt, Duke of Lancaster, the third son of King Edward III, and he had very large estates. When Henry of Derby was sent out of England, King Richard promised him that, if his father died, he should receive these estates.

King Richard reigned for two years more and he behaved in such a cruel way that everybody grew tired of him.

Deposition of Richard.

In 1399 old John of Gaunt died and King Richard broke his promise and took all his estates for himself. Then he went off to Ireland. While he was there he heard that his cousin, Henry, had landed in England to claim his estates. Richard hurried back and found that everybody was joining Henry and that nobody would help him. He was soon taken prisoner and brought to London. Parliament then forced him to resign and made his cousin king in his place as Henry IV. Soon after, King Richard died in prison. Nobody can be sorry for him for he threw away his kingdom by his own foolish conduct.

The Lollards.

It is in Richard's reign that we first hear of the Lollards. These men were the followers of a priest called John Wycliffe. Wycliffe was a religious reformer. He wanted to reform the Church for, he said, the priests were too wealthy and were not doing their work properly.

In those days England was covered with monasteries and many of these were very wealthy and had large estates. Wycliffe wanted all men to read the Bible for themselves. Up to that time it was written in Latin and could only be understood by educated people. Wycliffe translated it into English and sent men all over England to preach and to teach the people. But he and his followers were persecuted by the Church and were not allowed to carry out their scheme of reform.

Geoffrey Chaucer. Another famous man who lived at this period was Geoffrey Chaucer who is called the Father of English Poetry. At this time there were several dialects of English, the Northern, the Middle, and the Western. Chaucer wrote in Middle English and it is largely through him that this form of English became the general language of educated people all over England. His most famous poem is "Canterbury Tales" which is made up of a number of stories told by pilgrims on their way to the shrine of St. Thomas (Becket) at Canterbury.

CHAPTER VI

Lancaster and York.

King Henry IV 1399—1413.

With King Henry IV begins a new line of English kings—the House of Lancaster. King Henry had been put upon the throne by Parliament and, as the result of this, he and the other kings of his family were usually obliged to do what Parliament wished. King Henry was king, but he did not find it an easy task to govern the country. The friends of the late king soon started a rebellion. This failed and caused the death of Richard who had been kept a prisoner since he had been deposed. He was now so harshly treated in prison that he soon died. Then some of King Henry's own friends turned against him and started another rebellion with the help of the Welsh. King Henry managed to put this down after some hard fighting. But other rebellious followed and it was not until the last few years of his reign that he was free from such troubles. King Henry IV died in 1413 and was succeeded by his eldest son, King Henry V.

King Henry V 1413—1422.

In his youth the new King had been a wild young man, but when he became King he proved a very different person. He was a good soldier and he determined to win glory for himself and his family by making war on France again. And so he sent messengers to France demanding more land there and claiming the throne as his grandfather Edward III had done. France at the time was in a very disturbed state. The King was a weak-minded man who was often out of his senses, and there were two rival parties each trying to control the country.

Battle of Agincourt.

One of these parties headed by a great noble called the Duke of Burgundy promised to help King Henry. The French refused to do what Henry wished and so, in 1415, he led a great army over to France. After capturing one or two towns he found the French army in front of him at Agincourt and here, in October 1415 a great battle took place. Once again the English archers showed their skill and though the French were many more in number than the English they were badly beaten. After this battle Henry captured town after town till a great part of Normandy was in his hands. At last the French were obliged to make peace, by the Treaty of Troyes, in 1420. By this treaty Henry was to marry Katherine, the daughter of the French King, and upon the death of the latter was to become King of France.

Two years later, in 1422, King Henry died, rather suddenly, from dysentery. He was quite a young man but he was worn out with continual fighting. His wife had borne him a son in the year before and, as the French King died almost at the same time, the baby became King Henry VI of England and also King of France.

FRANCE
in 1429
English Miles
Lands recognising Henry VI
Lands recognising the Dauphin
Burgundian Lands
First campaign of Henry V
East from Greenwich
London
Oxford
Gloucester
Bristol
Canterbury
Dover
Southampton
Exeter
English Channel
Calais
FLANDERS
Ghent
Antwerp
Brussels
BRABANT
ARTOIS
Lille
Tournai
HAINAULT
Agincourt
Arras
Abbeville
Amiens
PICARDY
Compiegne
Cherbourg
Harfleur
Rouen
Honfleur
Beauvais
Caen
Soissons
Reims
Senlis
Meaux
Paris
NORMANDY
Verneuil
Corbeil
Melun
Fougeres
Chartres
BRITTANY
Rennes
MAINE
Patay
Orleans
Troyes
Sens
Quimperle
Vannes
Auxerre
Crevant
Dijon
Besancon
Angers
Tours
Blois
ANJOU
TOURAINE
Bourges
NEVERS
Nevers
BURGUNDY
(DUCHY)
(COUNTY)
Poitiers
POITOU
BERRY
BOURBON
SAVOY
BAY OF
BISCAY
Gironde
LIMOUSIN
Auvergne
Grenoble
DAUPHINE
Bordeaux
Dordogne
Lot
Tarn
Garonne
ARMAGNAC
Toulouse
PROVENCE
Durance
Bayonne
Adour
Pyrenees
Cevennes
Loire
Rhone
Saone
Isere
Allier
Vienne
Meuse
Moselle
Rhine
Somme
Seine
Marne
Domremy

MEDIAEVAL
ENGLAND & WALES
NORTH SEA
IRISH SEA
Cardigan Bay
Bristol Channel
ENGLISH CHANNEL
Isle of Man
CUMBERLAND
DURHAM
YORKSHIRE
LINCOLN
The Wash
NORFOLK
SUFFOLK
ESSEX
KENT
SURREY
WILTSHIRE
SOMERSET
DEVON
CORNWALL
DORSET
BERKSHIRE
HERTFORD
BEDFORD
CAMBRIDGE
NORTHAMPTON
LEICESTER
WARWICK
WORCESTER
STAFFORD
DERBY
SHROPSHIRE
HEREFORD
COUNTY PALATINE OF CHESTER
Bristol
London

King Henry VI 1422—1461.

As the new King was only a baby, a council was appointed to govern for him, while in France his uncle John, Duke of Bedford, took charge. The fighting still went on and, by 1429, nearly all the north of France was in English hands. But then there came a wonderful change.

Jeanne Darc.

Living in a small village in the east of France was a young peasant girl called Jeanne Darc. After a time Jeanne began to tell people that God and the saints had appeared to her in dreams and told her to go and save France. At first people did not believe her but after a time she persuaded an officer to take her to the place where Charles, the eldest son of the late French King, was living. Although she had never seen him before, she went straight up to him and told him that God had sent her to help him to become king. At that time the English were besieging the town of Orleans. Jeanne was given a suit of armour and, at the head of the French, who fought very bravely under her leadership, she saved the town from the English. Then she took Charles to Rheims and had him crowned King of France. Her work was now done and she wanted to go home, but the King kept her with him. At last she was captured and handed over to the English. In those days there were only two ideas about such a person as Jeanne. Either she was sent by God or she was a witch and was only fit to be punished. The English took the latter view. Jeanne was brought to trial and was burnt as a witch, at Rouen in 1431. 'We are lost, we have burnt a saint,' said an English soldier who saw the cruel deed. After her death she was made a saint and her memory is honoured to-day both by the English and the French.

Failure of the English.

The soldier had spoken the truth. The English were lost. Bedford died in 1435 and after his death, the English gradually lost everything. At last, in 1453, the long war came to an end and all that was left to England in France was the town of Calais.

The main reason for the English failure was the bad government in England. When Henry VI grew up he proved a very weak ruler. He was very pious, very kind, and very weak-minded and was quite the wrong kind of man to be king in those days. He married a French princess, Margaret of Anjou, a strong woman with a violent temper and she obtained such power over the King that he did everything she told him.

Madness of King Henry.

All over England people demanded that the country should be better governed, but the King took no notice and matters became worse as the war with France came to an end; for, the country was full of discharged soldiers, who had now nothing to do. At last the King became quite mad and then Parliament invited Richard, Duke of York, to become regent. Richard was a very able man and was really the rightful King, as he was descended from the second son of Edward III, Lionel Duke

LANCASTER AND YORK

of Clarence, while Henry VI was descended from John of Gaunt who was only the third son. For a few months York governed well. Then Henry recovered his senses and undid all the good that York had done. York then demanded that he should be made king on Henry's death, although Henry had a son of his own, Prince Edward.

The Wars of Roses.

Soon, in 1455, there broke out civil wars between the two parties, which are called the Wars of the Roses, from the badges of the two parties.

The Lancastrians, whose real leader was the Queen, took as their badge the red rose, while the Yorkists, whose leader was the Duke of York, wore the white rose.

At first the Yorkists were successful and took the King prisoner. Then the Lancastrians won the battle of Wakefield in 1460, in which the Duke of York was killed. York's claims to the throne passed to his eldest son Edward. Edward was assisted by a number of nobles, the chief of whom was Richard, Earl of Warwick, the most powerful man in England. With their help he defeated the Lancastrian armies and was crowned King as Edward IV in 1461. Henry VI was soon afterwards captured and put in the Tower of London where he remained for nine years. The Queen and her little son fled to France.

Edward IV 1461—1483.

The new king was the first King of the House of York. He was a tall, handsome man and was well liked by the people. For nine years he ruled in peace.

The King-Maker

Then trouble arose with the Earl of Warwick who had done so much to put Edward on throne that men called him the King-Maker. But he expected the King to do everything that he told him and grew angry when the King married a lady who was the widow of a Lancastrian, without telling him anything about it. He grew still more angry when the King surrounded himself with his wife's relations and took no notice of Warwick.

So the King-Maker made up his mind to make a new king. He went over to France and made friends with Queen Margaret and arranged a marriage between prince Edward and his daughter Then, in 1470, he invaded England. King Edward was caught by surprise and had to flee to Flanders. Warwick then took the poor old king Henry VI out of the Tower and made him king again. He was really quite senseless and simply did what he was told. But Edward IV soon came back and two great battles were fought. In the first, the battle of Barnet, the King-Maker was killed. He was too powerful a man to be a subject and England was well rid of him. In the second. the battle of Tewkesbury, the Queen's army was defeated and her son, Prince Edward, was captured and put to death. King Henry VI who had been put back into the Tower after the battle of Barnet was soon afterwards murdered. For the rest of his life King Edward ruled in peace. He died rather suddenly in 1483. His reign will always be famous for one thing—the introduction of printing

EDWARD IV VISITS THE CAXTON PRESS

into England. The art of printing had been invented some years before and, in 1476, William Caxton set up the first printing press in England.

King Edward V—1483.

The new King Edward V, the eldest son of the late King was only a lad and he did not reign long. Indeed he is the only King of England who was never crowned. His uncle, Richard, Duke of Gloucester, the younger brother of King Edward IV was an able but a cruel man. He wanted the throne for himself and so he started a story that his brother had never been properly married and that his son should not be king. In the end he persuaded the people to crown him as King Richard III. The poor little king and his brother Richard, Duke of York, were shut up in the Tower of London and were soon afterwards murdered by the orders of their cruel uncle! Many years afterwards, in the reign of Charles II, their bodies were found and were given proper burial.

King Richard III, 1483—1485.

King Richard had a short reign. He was hated for his cruelty and the murder of his two little nephews shocked the people. Soon a rival came to contest the crown with him. The main Lancastrian line died out with Prince Edward who was killed at Tewkesbury but Henry Tudor, Earl of Richmond, was descended from John of Gaunt, through his mother, Lady Margaret Beaufort. His claim was not very strong, for the Beaufort were illegitimate, but still he was a descendant of the Lancaster family. In 1485 he landed in Wales. His father.

Owen Tudor, was a Welshman and Henry counted on help from the Welsh. Many men joined him and he soon had a large army. King Richard hastened to meet him and the two armies met at Bosworth. Henry was victorious and King Richard fell fighting bravely to the last. His crown fell from his head when he was killed and it was picked up by one of Henry's friends who put it on his head and he was at once accepted as King Henry VII. With the accession of King Henry VII begins the modern period of English History.

CHAPTER VII

The Tudor Kings.

Henry VII 1485—1509.

The new King, Henry VII, proved a very successful ruler. His main work was to restore order in England after all the confusion of the Wars of the Roses. Most of the great lords had been killed in these wars. Those who were left were kept in order and were only allowed to have a limited number of men in their service. The case of the Earl of Oxford shows that the King meant this rule to be obeyed. Henry paid a visit to this nobleman, and, when the King was departing, a long line of men, dressed in Oxford's livery, was drawn up to do the King honour. King Henry thanked the Earl for his hospitality but fined him heavily, all the same, for breaking the rule. Cannon were now beginning to take the place of the old-fashioned weapons and King Henry took care that most of the cannon in England were in his control. He was very rich also as he possessed a great many estates, the owners of which had been killed in the wars.

In the early part of his reign he had a certain amount of trouble with pretenders. One of these, called Lambert Simnel, claimed to be the son of the Duke of Clarance brother of Edward IV. Henry disposed of him without much difficulty. The second, called Perkin Warbeck, gave him much more trouble. This young man pretended to be the younger of the two Princes murdered in the Tower and his story was believed by many. However, he, too, was defeated by Henry and shut up in the Tower, where he was afterwards put to death. In order to put an end to the strife between Lancaster and York, Henry married Elizabeth, the daughter of Edward IV, and took as his badge a double rose—red and white—to show that the two houses were now united.

Balance of power.

Henry took part in European politics also and in his reign we first hear of the idea of the 'balance of power' This means that it is not for the good of Europe that any one power should be very much stronger than the others. The rising power of Europe was Spain and so, to balance the power of France. Henry allied himself with Spain and married his eldest son, Arthur, to a Spanish princess, Catherine of Aragon. The young prince soon died and then his widow was married to his younger brother Henry.

The English in N. America.

In Henry's reign we first hear of an English expedition to the New World. Columbus had discovered America in 1492 and taken possession of it in the name of the King of Spain. In 1497 a sailor named Cabot was sent by Henry to explore further. But he sailed to the cold and foggy coast

THE LITTLE PRINCES IN THE TOWER

of Labrador and brought back such a gloomy story of that country that the English lost all interest in overseas discovery for many years.

Morton's Fork.

King Henry grew very greedy of money towards the end of his reign and this made him very unpopular. He was always trying to get money out of the people in all sorts of ways. One of his ministers, Morton, invented a plan called Morton's Fork because it caught both rich and poor. If a man appeared to be rich he was told he was spending too much and could afford to give some money to the King. If he seemed to be poor he was told he must be saving money and could therefore afford to give some to the King.

King Henry VII died in 1509. He found England in disorder, but he left it in good order and passed on a full treasury to his son.

Henry VIII 1509—1547.

The new King was a great contrast to his father. The old King had lived a very quiet and simple life. But the new King was a tall fine man, a very good athlete, and fond of all sorts of pleasures and amusements. He was also a good scholar and was also a composer of music. Some of his songs are still to be heard to-day.

Cardinal Wolsey.

For the first twenty-one years of his reign Henry worried very litle about the government. He spent all his time in amusements and left his clever minister, Cardinal Wolsey, to look after England. Wolsey was anxious to make England powerful in Europe, and persuaded his master to engage in a war with France without much result.

Henry's Divorce.

But in 1530 there came a change. We have seen how Henry had married his brother's widow, Catherine of Aragon. In those days such a marriage could only take place with the permission of Pope and the Pope had given this at the time. Henry above all things wanted a son but the Queen did not give him one. They had one daughter, Mary, and as years went on, it did not seem likely that the Queen would have any more children. And so Henry grew tired of her and wanted to marry someone else—one of her ladies called Anne Boleyn. The Pope was then the only person who could give him a divorce, so Henry applied for one. The Pope was in a difficult position. He did not want to make Henry angry by refusing. At the same time he did not want to offend Charles, King of Spain, who was the nephew of Queen Catherine.

The Reformation.

At this time the Pope and the Church were faced with great difficulties owing to the movement known as the Reformation. This had been started some years before in Germany by a monk called Martin Luther. Luther was a teacher in a university in Germany. In early days he had been a loyal supporter of the Church. Then he paid a visit to Rome and was very much disgusted at the state

HENRY VIII AND CARDINAL WOLSEY

of things there. He found that the leaders of the Church instead of leading pure and holy lives were spending their time in idle pleasure. This made him very sad and he went back to Germany where he soon began to attack the Church and the evils which he had seen in Rome. Luther, like Wycliffe in England at an earlier date, taught that there were many things in the Church that should be reformed. The movement spread in Germany and the north of Europe. Other men, more extreme than Luther, came to the front and in many countries the people broke away from the old Church altogether and formed new reformed churches. These people were known as Protestants because they protested against the teaching of the Church of Rome. Henry had written against Luther and his teaching, and the Pope had given him the title of 'Defender of the Faith' which is still borne by our Kings to-day.

Henry breaks with Rome.

After waiting for some time the Pope sent another Cardinal to England and told him to hear the King's case with the help of Wolsey. But they came to no decision and then Henry lost his temper. He turned Wolsey out of office and passed a number of laws which took away the authority of the Pope in England and put the King in his place. Other laws destroyed the old state of things altogether and set up a new form of Church in England. Many great and good men could not agree to these changes, and Henry treated them very cruelly and put many of them to death with the help of his new minister, a stern, hard man called Thomas Cromwell.

The Monasteries.

At that time England was covered with monasteries some of which were very rich. These monasteries had done very useful work in earlier days. The monks were skilled in medicine and had hospitals where the sick could be treated. They also maintained guest rooms where travellers could spend the night for in those days there were few inns in the country Many of the monks too were skilful farmers and taught the people better methods of cultivating the land. They were historians also and much of our knowledge of those times is derived from chronicles written in the monasteries. But the need for the monasteries was gone and many of the monks had grown lazy from having nothing to do. So far back as the reign of Henry VII when his mother Lady Margaret Beaufort, who was a very pious woman, wished to give her money to the monasteries, she was advised not to do so but to found colleges at Cambridge instead as being more useful. Cardinal Wolsey himself had shut up some of the smaller monasteries and taken their money to found a college at Oxford. Henry hated the monks because they supporteed the Pope. So, under Cromwell's direction, all sorts of accusations were brought against them. They were turned out of their monasteries and their lands and money were either seized by the King himself or given to his friends.

Anne Boleyn.

Now that he had broken with the Pope, Henry made up his mind to get rid of his wife himself. So he persuaded Cranmer, the Archbishop of Canterbury, who was a supporter of the King's policy, to grant him a divorce. Henry then married Anne Boleyn who soon bore him a daughter, Elizabeth. But she gave him no son and Henry soon grew tired of her. So he made up his mind to get rid of her. She was accused of behaving improperly and was put to death. Henry then married his third wife, Jane Seymour, who bore him a son, in 1537, but died a few days afterwards.

Henry's other wives.

In 1540 he married again—this time a German princess named Anne of Cleves. Cromwell had persuaded Henry to do this in order that he might have the help of the Protestant princes of Germany against the Pope. But Henry did not like Anne of Cleves at all and soon got rid of her, and Cromwell, who had arranged the marriage, was put to death in 1540. Henry VIII married two more wives before his death. One of them—Katherine Howard was found guilty of improper conduct and put to death. The other, Catherine Parr, survived him.

As he grew older Henry grew more and more cruel and everyone was terrified of him. He became extremely fat and suffered for many years from a horrible disease. At last he died in 1547. The most important event of his reign is the breaking of the old connection between England and the Pope.

King Edward VI, 1547—1553.

The new King was a delicate little boy of ten and the government was in the hands of the Council, the chief man being the King's uncle, Edward Seymour, Duke of Somerset. Somerset was a well-meaning man but he made many mistakes. He tried to force the Scots to marry their young queen to his nephew and, when they refused, made war upon them. The only result was that the Scots sent away their young queen to France to be brought up there. Soon Somerset was turned out and not long afterwards put to death. His place as chief man in the Council was taken by John Dudley—Duke of Northumberland—a scheming and ambitious man. Both Somerset and Northumberland pushed on the Reformation in England and made a great many changes in the church. But Northumberland now went still further. The young King was in very bad health and was not likely to live long. He was a keen supporter of the Reformation and of the various changes that had been made. Northumberland now persuaded him to make a will by which he set aside his two sisters, Mary and Elizabeth, and left the crown to his cousin, Lady Jane Grey, who, like the King, was a supporter of the changes in religion. Northumberland had married his son, Lord Guildford Dudley, to this lady so that if she became queen, he would be the chief man in the Council. Not long afterwards the young King died in 1553.

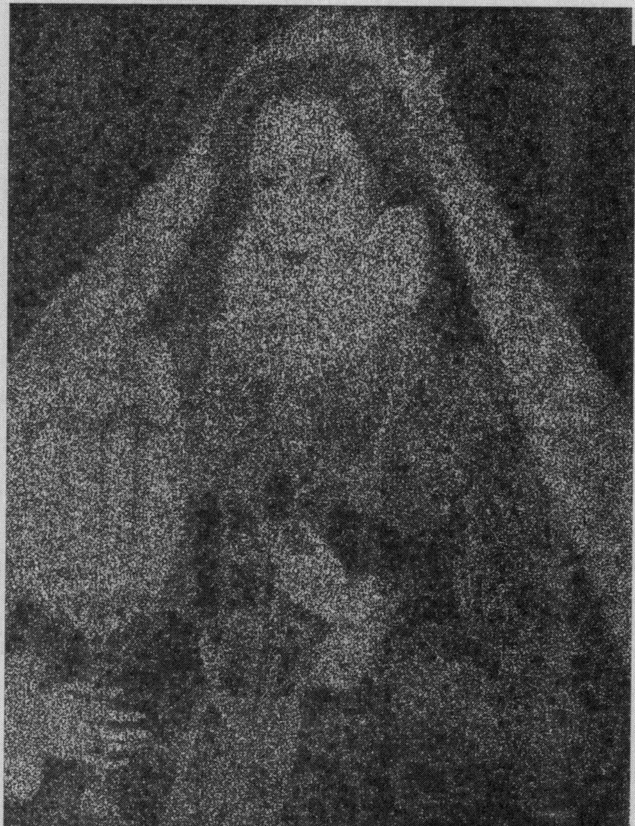

QUEEN ELIZABETH

CHAPTER VIII

The Tudor Queens.

Mary 1553—1558.

As soon as King Edward was dead, Northumberland tried to carry out his plan. He made Lady Jane Queen and forced the Council to agree. But his scheme soon failed. All over England the people rose in favour of Queen Mary, whom they held was the rightful Queen. Soon Northumberland found himself alone. He then tried to change sides, but it was too late. Mary came up to London in triumph and was crowned Queen. Northumberland was put on his trial and soon afterwards beheaded. Poor Lady Jane and her husband were put into the Tower.

The new Queen was a strong supporter of the old religion and she at once began to undo all that had been done. She wished to start the monasteries again, but this could not be done, as their lands and money had been given away to other people who would not give them back again.

Mary's marriage.

Mary was very anxious also to bring England once more under the control of the Pope and, to help her to do this, she married Philip II of Spain, the most powerful Roman Catholic King of the time. People in England did not like this marriage at all and there was a rebellion headed by a man called Sir Thomas Wyatt. This did not succeed and the only result was to cause the death of poor Lady Jane and her husband who were now put to death. The fate of Lady Jane is a very sad one. She was a good, clever, and innocent girl who was made the tool of the schemes of Northumberland.

Persecution of the Protestant.

Soon after Mary's marriage with Philip, England was once more united to Rome. Mary then began to treat very cruelly all those who would not give up the new religion. We must not blame her too much. All over Europe the same thing was going on and her husband Philip was killing hundreds of the Protestants in Holland which was then under his rule. Nearly 300 people were burnt in England for refusing to give up the Protestant religion. Some were very important people, such as Cranmer, the Archbishop of Canterbury, and Bishops Ridley and Latimer. "Be of good comfort," said Latimer, as he and Ridley stood side by side at the stake at Oxford. "We shall this day light such a candle, by God's grace in England, as I trust shall never be put out." Others were quite humble folk but all died bravely for their faith. The cruel treatment of these people made Mary hated by nearly everybody. Mary's marriage proved very unhappy. Philip was a cold, hard man and soon after the marriage he went back to Europe and hardly ever came near Mary again. Mary was very anxious to have a child who might be brought up in her religion. But no child was born to her and she knew that her sister, Elizabeth, who would be queen after her, was in favour of the Protestant religion.

Loss of Calais.

Soon Mary's health began to fail. At this time war broke out between France and Spain and England was obliged to take part. Then came the news that the French had taken Calais, the last English possession in France. At the time it seemed a great disaster. But really it was a good thing for England. As long as Calais was English there was always a chance that England might one day win back her lost lands in France. But the loss of Calais caused this idea to be given up altogether and made Englishmen look in a new place—over the seas—for their future greatness.

The news of the fall of Calais proved a great shock to Mary. "When I die," she said, "Calais will be found written on my heart." Not long after, in 1558, she passed away. It was a sad end to a sad life.

Elizabeth 1558—1603.

The new Queen was a great contrast to her sister. Mary was old, and in bad health. Elizabeth was a fine young woman, fond of bright clothes and dancing and all kinds of amusement. The reign of Elizabeth is a very important one in English history because it saw the beginning of England's world power. Up to that time England had been merely a European power and not always a very important one. But the great sailors who lived under

Elizabeth made the beginning of the British Empire and gave England her first possessions over the seas.

The Church of England.

The first question that Elizabeth had to settle was that of religion. She herself was in favour of the Protestant religion and she found that most people were in favour of it also. The cruelties of Mary's reign had made people hate the Roman Catholics. So an Act was passed which set up a new national church called the Church of England of which the Queen was to be the head. Elizabeth hoped that everybody would agree to this as the new Church was a mixture of the old and the new. It kept many of the old ceremonies, but also took in many of the changes made by the Reformation. Unfortunately there were two classes of people who would not join the new Church. These were the old Roman Catholics who wanted no change at all, and the extreme Protestants who thought the new Church was too much like the old one. These extreme Protestants were called Puritans. As they demanded freedom in religious matters. they soon began to demand it in political affairs also. It was the Puritans who took the leading part in the great struggle between King and Parliament in the next century, which ended in what is often called as the "civil war" but which is better described as the "Puritan Rebellion."

The Virgin Queen.

These changes put Elizabeth in great danger. The Pope declared that she was a heretic and ordered the Roman

ELIZABETH SIGNING MARY STUART'S DEATH-WARRANT

Catholic powers to turn her out. Luckily for her the two chief Roman Catholic powers, France and Spain, were on such bad terms that they would not join against her. Hence she could play them off one against the other and it was for this reason that she probably never married and is known as the "Virgin Queen." As long as she did not marry she could always propose to marry a French or a Spanish prince. On the whole she took the side of France, for France was a less dangerous enemy than Spain.

Mary Queen of Scots.

Elizabeth's difficulties were made greater by affairs in Scotland. The Scots had most of them become extreme Protestants but their Queen, Mary, was a Roman Catholic. Now Mary was Elizabeth's cousin, for her grandmother, Margaret, was a sister of Henry VIII. The Roman Catholics in England considered that Mary was the rightful Queen of England, for they did not consider that Henry VII had any right to get rid of his first wife, Catherine of Aragon, and that therefore his marriage to Anne Boleyn, the mother of Elizabeth, was not a real marriage at all. In 1569 there was trouble in Scotland. Mary was driven out by her people who believed she had been mixed up in the murder of her husband, a foolish man called Lord Darnley. Driven out of Scotland she took refuge in England. It was difficult to know what to do with her. In the end she was kept as a prisoner and remained so for 18 years—till 1587

The Great English Sailors.

During these years England and Spain became greater and greater enemies. For one thing the English Protestants went over to help the Dutch in their struggle against Philip. Then there was also the question of the New World. Spain and Portugal claimed most of America between them. But a race of English sailors was growing up who began to make voyages to the New World and to make war on the Spaniards there. Whenever the Spaniards caught any of them they burnt them as heretics, so the war really became a religious one.

There were some very famous men among these English sailors and we must give some account of them and their deeds. Sir John Hawkins is best known as the first man to start the Slave Trade—that is the carrying over of African negroes to the New World as slaves. Sir Walter Raleigh, another famous sailor, founded the first English Colony in North America which he called Virginia in honour of the Virgin Queen. From America he brought over to Europe tobacco and the potato. His brother-in-law, Sir Humphrey Gilbert, discovered Newfoundland in 1583—the oldest of the British Colonies. The most famous of them all was Sir Francis Drake who was the first Englishman to sail round the world. He took three years to do this starting in 1577 and returning in 1580. These men made the name of England feared wherever they went.

FRANCIS DRAKE

Death of Mary.

During all these years Mary Queen of Scots remained a prisoner in England. Plot after plot was formed by the Roman Catholics to kill Elizabeth and put Mary on the throne. But Elizabeth's clever ministers, Cecil and Walsingham, knew all that was going on. At last, in 1587 a very dangerous plot was discovered in which Mary was mixed up. Then her ministers told Elizabeth that she would never be safe until Mary was dead. Elizabeth did not want to put her cousin to death but at last she consented and Mary was beheaded at Fotheringay Castle in 1587.

The Armada.

When Philip of Spain heard of this he declared war and started fitting out a great expedition against England called the Spanish Armada. While this was being prepared Drake sailed to Spain and destroyed a great part of it. However, in the summer of 1588, the Armada came to England. The English fleet was commanded by Lord Howard of Effingham; and Drake, Raleigh, and all the other great English sailors were serving under him. When the news of the coming of the Armada reached England most of the English ships were at Plymouth and Drake and some of the English captains were on shore, playing bowls. The others wished to go back to their ships at once but Drake said "No! There is plenty of time to finish our game first and beat the Spaniards afterwards." In a number of fights in the English Channel the English sailors did great damage to the Spaniards. In the end, the Spanish fleet took refuge in the harbour of Calais. It had been arranged that a Spanish army from the Netherlands should join them and be carried over to conquer England. But the English sent fire-ships into the harbour and the Spaniards were forced to come out in confusion into the open sea. Then a storm came on and the Spanish Armada was blown far away north where most of the ships were wrecked on the coast of Scotland and England. Of 153 ships only 53 got back to Spain. The defeat of the Armada had two important results. It gave the English the command of the sea and so enabled them to build up their Empire. It also made Holland a nation, for Spain could no longer send troops to conquer the Dutch.

For the rest of her reign Elizabeth had much less trouble. England was too strong to be attacked, and, after the death of Philip in 1598, Spain began to grow weaker.

End of the reign.

The latter part of the reign will always be famous for the rise of William Shakespeare—one of the greatest poets in the world. From his plays we get a very good idea of the point of view of the Englishmen of the days of Elizabeth, and we see a new English nationality beginning. Religion had a good deal to do with this, for religion in England was now a national thing. Not long before the end of her reign Elizabeth granted a Charter to the East India Company, in 1600, and English expansion began in the East as well as in the West.

THE SPANISH ARMADA IN THE ENGLISH CHANNEL

Elizabeth was now getting an old woman and her health began to fail. At last in 1603 the long reign came to an end. As Elizabeth left no children the crown now passed to her cousin, James, the son of Mary Queen of Scots. He had ruled in Scotland for a number of years as James VI and he now became James I of England. With his coronation in Westminster Abbey upon the famous stone of Scone the old saying came true that wherever the stone went Scots Kings would reign.

CHAPTER IX

The First Stuart King.

James I 1603—1625.

As we have seen in our last chapter Queen Elizabeth was succeeded by her cousin James Stuart. James had been King of Scotland as James VI for a number of years and he now became James I of England as well. In those days the English regarded the Scots as foreigners—indeed it was only a few years since the two nations had been at war with one another. Hence James was not very popular in his new kingdom, nor did he make things any better by his own conduct and appearance. The Tudor sovereigns had been good rulers and had been full of personal dignity. James I had none of the latter. He was an ill-built, undignified figure with a rolling walk, and with a tongue too big for his mouth which made his speech absurd. He was a coward also and trembled at the sight of a sword.

James' Favourites.

He was a great reader and also a writer of books and was very proud of his knowledge. But he made such bad use of it that men called him the 'wisest fool in Christendom.' He brought with him from Scotland a number of his Scots friends most of whom were very poor and he made himself much disliked by the large grants of land and money which he gave to them. Further he was always in the hands of favourites—first of a Scotsman, Robert Carr, whom he made Earl of Somerset and then of an Englishman, George Villiers, Duke of Buckingham—and he would do nothing without their advice. Even his ministers had to go to the favourites if they wanted the King to do anything.

James came to the throne at a very difficult time, when even a capable king would have found it hard to rule. A king like James only made things very much worse.

James' Difficulties.

There were two main difficulties at the time—the position of Parliament and the question of religion. The Tudor sovereigns had been very absolute in their rule but they had been very careful to consult Parliament and during their time, particularly in the latter part of Elizabeth's long reign, Parliament began to feel its power. It was rather like a child which grows from infancy into childhood and then into youth. A wise parent will realize the change and as the child grows up will gradually give him more and more freedom. A foolish parent, however, who still tries to treat the youth as a child will only cause him to rebel. James was of the latter class and instead of giving Parliament more power was for ever interfering with it. He made long speeches telling Parliament what a wise man he was and how he was king by the will of God and that no one should disobey him. This only annoyed the members of Parliament and when he followed this up by all sorts of illegal actions, he started a rebellious feeling which came to ahead in the days of his son Charles I.

There was also the question of religion. Elizabeth had set up the Church of England in the hope that it would please everybody. But two classes would have nothing to do with it. The Roman Catholics remained faithful to the old religion, while the extreme Protestants, who were called Puritans or Non-conformists, disliked the Church of England as being too much like that of Rome and wished to worship in their own way.

The Puritans.

Being independent in their religious views they became independent in their political views also and it was largely this class who opposed the King in Parliament. As soon as he came to England, James I, who fancied himself a great authority on religion, tried to reconcile the Non-conformists to the Church of England. For this purpose he called a conference of the leaders of both parties and tried to arrange a settlement. But nothing came of this. The Non-conformists demanded many changes which the Church would not grant and the only result of the conference was a new English translation of the Bible (1611)—called the Authorized Version—which continued to be in regular use till a new translation was prepared in the reign of Queen Victoria (1881).

As James' mother, Mary Queen of Scots, had been a Roman Catholic, the members of that church hoped that James would do something for them and would take away some of the harsh laws which had been passed against them. But James would do nothing.

Gunpowder Plot.

Some of the more violent among the Roman Catholics then made a plot to murder the King and his Parliament. This is the famous Gunpowder Plot which took place in 1605.

It was so called because the scheme was to fill a cellar underneath the Houses of Parliament with gunpowder and to blow up the Houses while Parliament was sitting.

Everything was ready and a man called Guy Fawkes was to go down to the cellar and set fire to the powder. But the plot failed as one of the conspirators wishing to save his cousin who was a member of the House of Lords sent him an anonymous letter of warning. Search was at once made and Guy Fawkes was caught in the cellar. He and most of the other conspirators were put to death. The plot so frightened James that he only persecuted the Roman Catholics worse than before. The day of the discovery of the plot, November 5, Guy Fawkes day, as it is called, is still commemorated in England. The schoolboys make straw images of Guy Fawkes which they carry in procession round the town and which are finally burnt in the evening—rather like the burning of Ravan in the Ram Lila ceremony in India.

Foreign Policy.

James was a coward and feared war. As soon as he could do so he made peace with Spain and wanted to ally himself with that country. People in England, who remembered the glorious deeds of the great seamen of Elizabeth's reign, did not like this at all. Only one of these great seamen was still alive—Sir Walter Raleigh. James accused him of conspiring against him and put him in the Tower for many years. Then he allowed him to go to South America to search for gold. He failed to get any gold and when he came back James put him to death, mainly to please the Spaniards who complained that he had attacked their colonies. It was a sad end to a great career.

James and Parliament.

James' main trouble all through his reign was lack of money and most of his quarrels with Parliament were over this question. When Parliament refused to give him any more he dismissed it and set about raising money in all sorts of illegal ways. His opponents tried to stop this by taking matters into the law courts. But as in those days the judges were appointed and paid by the king they were afraid to go against his wishes and so they gave their decisions in the king's favour.

The lack of money was not entirely the fault of the King. It is true that he gave away far too much to his favourites. But, apart from this, the value of money had fallen, as silver was now much cheaper. Hence the King found it very difficult to manage on the same amount as Elizabeth had done. The Parliament did not understand the difficulty and, when the King asked for more money, only protested and said that the King ought to be able to manage with what he had.

Prince Henry.

James was married to Anne of Denmark and by her he had two sons and a daughter. It was a great misfortune that his eldest son, Henry, died in 1612 when he was only 18. He was a very promising young man, and much more tolerant than his father in his religious views. Had he lived he would probably have made a very good king and much of the trouble that came afterwards might have been stopped. As it was, his younger brother, Charles, a far less able man, came to the throne. The daughter, Elizabeth, was married to a German prince, Frederick of the Palatinate.

James was very anxious to maintain the friendship with Spain and wished his son, Charles, to marry a Spanish princess. But the Spaniards would give no definite answer, for they did not wish a Spanish princess to marry a Protestant At last Charles and the King's favourite, the Duke of Buckingham, went over to Spain to try and arrange the marriage. But the Spaniards were angry at this and Charles and the favourite came back in disgust.

Not long after this, in 1625, James I died. His reign was full of mistakes and foolish actions and the troubles which occurred in the reign of his son were largely due to him.

Shakespeare and Bacon.

Two great names in English literature are connected with this reign. Shakespeare, who had begun to write his plays in the days of Elizabeth, wrote many more in the reign of James and died in 1616. Francis Bacon also lived in this period. He was probably the cleverest man of his time in Europe and his writings on philosophy and many other subjects are well known.

Beginning of the Empire.

The reign of James also saw the beginning of the British Colonies. In 1625 Barbados, the oldest Colony in the West Indies, was acquired by England. Raleigh had founded Virginia in the reign of Elizabeth but there was no real settlement there till 1607. Further Colonies in America were founded at this time by Puritans who, tired of persecution in England, left their homes to settle in the New World. The first of these were known as the Pilgrim Fathers. In 1620 in a little ship—the famous Mayflower—they sailed across the Atlantic and founded a new home in America which they called Plymouth. Later on other Puritans joined them and this group of Colonies came to be known as New England.

WILLIAM SHAKESPEARE

CHAPTER X

Charles I.

The new King was a much better man than his father. He was a religious man and a man of purity and refinement. At any other time he might have made a very good king. But he was weak, and like all weak men, he was very obstinate. From his father he had learned a good deal that was bad and when he became King he had not the sense to make any changes but continued to act in the same foolish way that his father had done.

Charles I 1625—1642.

Soon after he became King, he married a French princess, Henrietta Maria. She had great influence over him and many of his foolish acts were the result of her advice.

For the first few years of his reign Charles was very much under the influence of Buckingham. The latter was very much disliked by Parliament and, when the King called Parliament together to get money, all sorts of charges were brought against Buckingham. To save his friend, Charles got rid of the Parliament but, as he was badly in need of money, he was soon forced to call another in 1628. This Parliament drew up a statement called the Petition of Right, which was a list of illegal acts that had

Buckingham.

been committed by Charles and his father. The chief complaints were that people had been forced to pay money to the King without the consent of Parliament and that many people had been put into prison without proper trial in the courts, a thing which had been forbidden by the Great Charter in the reign of John. The King was obliged to promise that he would not do any of these things in future, before Parliament gave him any money.

Soon after this Buckingham was murdered by a man who had a grievance against him.

Strafford.

Charles now found a new adviser in Sir Thomas Wentworth whom he afterwards made Earl of Strafford. Wentworth had been a member of Parliament and had been opposed to the King until after the Petition of Right. Wentworth thought that the King had done enough in agreeing to this Petition and, when the more violent members wanted to go further and to cut down the King's power still more, Wentworth left them and went over to the King. He was a strong, hard man and his motto was 'Thorough.' He believed that the only way to govern the country properly was for the King to have the chief power and to govern through a strong Minister like himself. The Puritan members hated Wentworth. A man who changes sides is always unpopular with those whom he has left. "You have left us, but we will never leave you while you have a head on your shoulders" said one of the Puritan leaders.

In the year after the Petition of Right, 1629, Parliament met again and once more complained that the King was acting wrongly and was collecting money in all sorts of improper ways. It was the old story of want of money. The King had not enough of it to govern the country properly and Parliament would not give him any more without binding him down by all sorts of conditions to which he could not agree. As neither side would give way, Charles dismissed the Parliament and for eleven years, till 1640, he governed without one. During these years, as the King had to get money somehow, he collected it in all sorts of ways which only made him more unpopular. Wentworth also was hated by the Puritan party for they believed that Charles was doing all this on his advice.

Ship Money.

The best known case of the way in which the King tried to collect money was that of Ship Money. Ship Money was a very old tax which was laid upon the counties on the coast. The money so collected was intended to be spent upon ships to protect the coast. Charles now said that as the ships protected the whole country, the inland counties should pay as well. The Puritan leaders were very angry at this and one of them, John Hampden, refused to pay. The case was heard in the courts and the judges decided in favour of the King.

Charles' policy in matters of religion also

Laud. made him very unpopular. He was a strong supporter of the Church of England and in 1633 he made William Laud Archbishop of Canterbury. Laud was a good man but he could only see one point of view. He introduced a great many changes which made the services in the Church of England much more like those of the Church of Rome. The Puritans naturally did not like this but when they protested Laud would not listen to them. He was strongly supported by Charles and the latter allowed him to punish and persecute all those who would not accept the changes which he had made.

Church of Scotland. Not content with making changes in the Church of England, Laud persuaded the King that he should make changes in the Church of Scotland also. The Scots were extreme Protestants and their religion was called Presbyterianism. In this form of Christianity there were no bishops and no regular prayer-book. Charles now ordered that the Scots should use the same prayer-book as that in use in England. The Scots refused to do this and broke into rebellion in 1639. Charles was therefore forced to send an army against them. But he had no money to fit out his soldiers properly and had to make peace. Early in 1640 Charles called together a new Parliament and asked for money. But the Parliament demanded so much from the King before it would give him anything that he dismissed it after a few weeks. This

The Great Council.

The war with Scotland broke out again and Charles tried a new way of raising money. He called together a great Council of all the leading nobles. Such a Council had not met for many years. Before Parliament came into existence in 1295 such councils had often met but now all their power had been taken over by Parliament. All that the Council could do was to advise the King to call another Parliament. In the meantime, the Scots had again beaten the King's army and he was obliged to make peace.

The Long Parliament.

In November 1640 Charles called together a new Parliament, the famous Long Parliament, so called because it lasted for 19 years, and it did not finally come to an end till 1659.

As soon as the Long Parliament met the Puritans attacked their chief enemy Strafford They could not prove anything against him, so they brought in a bill saying that he ought to be put to death. Charles was a long time in making up his mind to agree to this but at last he did so and Strafford was executed in 1641. The many misfortunes which afterwards fell upon the King were a just punishment for consenting to the death of his faithful adviser.

The Puritans did not forget their other enemy, the Archbishop of Canterbury. He too was arrested and thrown into prison, though it was some years before he was put to death.

many changes. To some of them Charles agreed, to others he could not. Finally Parliament drew up a long list of grievances called the Grand Remonstrance and tried to force the King to accept it. This he could not do, for, if he had done so, he would have had no power at all left.

Charles attacks Parliament.

Soon after this Charles foolishly attempted to arrest the leaders of the Puritan party as they sat in the House of Commons. But they were warned in time and managed to get away before the King and his soldiers came. This was a foolish act, for the members of the House of Commons have always claimed the privilege of "freedom of speech." That is to say, a man may say what he likes in the House and cannot be punished for it outside. Charles in coming to Parliament and trying to arrest the leaders showed that he had no respect for their old privilege.

Beginning of War.

The quarrel between the King and his Parliament could now only be settled by fighting and both sides began to prepare for war. In August 1642 Charles set up his standard at Nottingham and called upon his people to help him to subdue his rebellious Parliament. Then begins what is sometimes called the civil war but what is better called the Puritan Rebellion. It was as much religious as political. Indeed the King had already granted most of the more reasonable demands of the Puritans so far as government was concerned.

But the Puritans hated the Church of England

and the King and his party stood for the Church. Hence it was largely to destroy the Church that the Puritans rebelled against their King.

Expansion of the Empire.

While all these troubles were going on in England, the expansion of Colonies still went on. In 1628 the island of Nevis in the West Indies had been occupied. In 1629 another party of Puritans founded the Colony of Massachusetts in New England. In 1632 the group of island in the West Indies called the Leeward Islands was occupied. In 1634 another American colony was founded, this time for Roman Catholics. The new colony received the name of Maryland in honour of the Queen.

In India the East India Company also was making progress. The factory at Surat had been founded in 1611, and in 1633 came the first factory in Bengal. Six years later, in 1639, Madras was acquired by purchase and a factory of the Company was placed there also.

CHAPTER XI

The Puritan Rebellion and the Commonwealth.

The Puritan Rebellion.

In the war which now broke out the King had at first all the advantage. Most of the north, centre, and south-west of England took his side, while the chief strength of the Parliament lay in London and the eastern counties. The King's forces were called the Cavaliers. They were mounted men—cavalier means horseman—and were countrymen, used to riding and shooting. Hence they naturally made better soldiers than the townsmen who composed the bulk of the army of the Parliament. The latter were called Roundheads by their opponents. In those days it was the fashion to wear the hair long and flowing down over the shoulders. But the Puritans disapproved of this and cut their hair short, as we do to-day. Hence the name Roundhead was given to them as a term of contempt.

Early Stages.

The King made his headquarters at Oxford during the early part of the war; although he tried to take London, he was not able to do so. The principal battles in the early part of the war were founght at Edgehill and Newbury. In these battles the Cavaliers had a slight advantage. The Parliamentary party now turned to the Scots for help and made a treaty with them by which the Scots promised to come to their help. In the meantime a new leader was coming to the front on the side of the Parliament who was in the end to win the war for them. This was Oliver Cromwell.

Oliver Cromwell.

Oliver Cromwell was a country gentleman from the eastern counties and had been a member of Parliament. He soon saw that the Parliament would never be successful as long as their armies were composed of the people of the towns, who did not make good soldiers. Hence he set himself to train men from his own part of the country and, although he had never been a soldier before, he showed himself such a good leader that his soldiers soon became the best of those which the Parliament had. They were called the Ironsides and Cromwell was very careful to pick men of good character who were keen Puritans and who felt that in fighting against the Cavaliers they were doing a religious duty. In 1643, the second year of the war, Cromwell won his first victory over the Cavaliers at Winceby, in which the Ironsides showed they were better men than their opponents.

Success of the Parliament.

In 1644 came the first great victory of the Parliamentary army—the battle of Marston Moor. The Roundheads were besieging York—the chief city of the north of England—and a Scots' army was coming down to join them. The King's army under his nephew Rupert came up from the south to prevent this and joined up with the garrison of York. The battle was fought at Marston Moor, a few miles from York, and the victory was mainly due to Cromwell's Ironsides who broke to pieces the division of the Royalists in front of them. "God made them as stubble before our swords" wrote Cromwell to a friend. After this battle the strength of the King's party began to grow less. On the advice of Cromwell the Parliament re-organized their army on what was called the New Model. The useless old soldiers were got rid of and their place was taken by carefully picked men of strong religious views like Cromwell's own men. Cromwell himself was given a high command in the new army.

Naseby.

In 1645 the Parliament won the great victory of Naseby which was again largely due to Cromwell. This battle really ended the war as the King's army was destroyed. To make things worse all his private papers were captured and from these it was discovered that the Queen, who had gone to France with her children, was trying to get soldiers and money from the French. This only made the Parliament hate the King more than before. In 1646 Charles in despair gave himself up to the Scots' army. But the Scots would not help him and in 1647 handed him over to the Parliament for a sum of £400,000. He soon passed into the hands of the army who were beginning to quarrel with Parliament and to take matters into their own hands. Many of the members of Parliament

ENGLAND
during the
CIVIL WAR
English Miles
SCOTLAND
Firth of Forth
Stirling
Dumbarton
Glasgow
Berwick
Kelso
Selkirk
Philiphaugh
Newcastle
Tyne
Carlisle
Durham
Solway Firth
Penrith
Appleby
Barnard Castle
Richmond
Kendal
Ravenglass
Scarborough
Isle of Man
Castletown
Bolton Castle
NORTH
SEA
IRISH SEA
York
Beverley
Hull
Humber
Preston
Skipton
Wakefield
Ribble
Ormskirk
Wigan
Sandal Castle
Pontefract
Doncaster
Liverpool
Manchester
Retford
Sheffield
Lincoln
Chester
Conway
Denbigh
Carnarvon
Holt
Wrexham
Nantwich
Southwell
Newark
Boston
The Wash
Nottingham
Uttoxeter
Derby
Market Drayton
Stafford
Belvoir Castle
Oswestry
Shrewsbury
Lichfield
Ashby de la Zouch
King's Lynn
Norwich
Crowland
Cardigan Bay
Leicester
Montgomery
Ludlow
Coventry
Naseby
Huntingdon
Ely
Warwick
Northampton
Newmarket
Bury St. Edmunds
Cambridge
Ipswich
Towcester
Bedford
Malvern
Cardigan
Hereford
Banbury
Tewkesbury
Colchester
Haverford west
Carmarthen
Abergavenny
Gloucester
St. Albans
Chelmsford
Raglan
Oxford
Chepstow
Abingdon
Wallingford
Watford
Pembroke
Uxbridge
London
Cardiff
Malmesbury
Thames
Bristol
Windsor
Richmond
Maidstone
Bristol Channel
Bath
Wells
Andover
Basing
Canterbury
Barnstaple
Bridgwater
Farnham
Dover
Taunton
Langport
Salisbury
Winchester
Horsham
Torrington
Tiverton
Southampton
Chichester
Brighton
Chard
Blandford
Crediton
Exeter
Poole
Portsmouth
Dorchester
Carisbrooke Castle
Launceston
Tavistock
Wight
Bodmin
Liskeard
Exe
St. Austell
Plymouth
Truro
Dartmouth
ENGLISH CHANNEL

were Presbyterians and were disliked by Cromwell and his soldiers, most of whom belonged to the extreme Puritan party and were called Independents.

War with Scotland.

This brought about a quarrel between them and the Scots, who were Presbyterians, and the Scots now took up the cause of the King and invaded England in 1648. This is called the second civil war. Cromwell marched against the Scots and defeated them at Preston. All this time Charles had remained in prison in different places. Had he been a wise man he might have succeeded in becoming King again, as both Parliament and the army were willing to have him back upon their own conditions. But he tried to play them one against the other till neither side would trust him. At last Cromwell and the army made up their minds to get rid of him altogether. They had now got Parliament into their power by turning out all the Presbyterian members and keeping only those who belonged to their own party—the Independents. The King was brought up to London and put on trial before a court of judges set up by the army. Of course this was quite wrong, for such a court had no right to try the King. But as the army had all the power in their own hands they were able to do as they liked.

Charles. Execution of

Charles behaved bravely and calmly before his judges and merely said that they had no right to try a King. Many people said that the King was quite right but they were afraid of the army and could do nothing. Charles was found guilty of making war upon his people and sentenced to death. On January 30, 1649, he was beheaded outside his own palace of Whitehall. In his last speech the King declared that he died for the cause of the Church of England and he was quite right. The war had become a religious war—a struggle between the Puritans and the Church—and for the time being the Puritans had won the day. But the execution of the King shocked a great many people, as did also the Puritan treatment of the Church. They damaged and destroyed the churches, pulling down images and breaking beautiful windows and ornaments and this did not make them popular. Because of these things people looked on the King as a martyr and he is sometimes called King Charles the Martyr.

The Commonwealth, 1649—1660.

The remains of the Parliament now declared that England should have no king in future, but should be a republic—the Commonwealth as it was called. The period may be divided into two parts, the first part ending in 1653. During these years Parliament attempted to govern the country. Cromwell, now the chief man in England, was busy elsewhere. During the war King Charles had obtained much help from the Irish. Now the Irish were largely Roman Catholics and Cromwell and the Independents regarded them as worse than infidels. Hence as soon as he could, Cromwell crossed over to Ireland with his army. He de-

CHARLES I ON HIS WAY TO EXECUTION.

feated the Irish and took several of their towns, behaving with fearful cruelty towards the people. He then turned out most of the native Irish and gave their land to English settlers. Cromwell's cruel deeds in Ireland were really the beginning of the bad feeling between England and Ireland which lasted for so many years and to this day the memory of Cromwell is hated by the Irish. When he finished the subduing of the Irish, Cromwell turned his attention to Scotland. Scotland was still at war with England and Cromwell now led an English army to the north.

Cromwell in Scotland.

The Scots' army met him at Dunbar on September 2, 1651 and more by good luck than by anything else, Cromwell managed to defeat them. But the war was not yet over. The Scots had brought over Charles, the elder son of the late King and had crowned him as King of Scotland. In the next year, 1651, the Scots' army invaded England bringing their King with them. Cromwell met them at Worcester and utterly defeated them. King Charles fled to the south and managed to escape to France after many narrow escapes. On one occasion he was actually hidden among the boughs of an oak tree while Cromwell's soldiers were standing underneath.

War with the Dutch.

During the war England had lost most of her power in Europe and Cromwell with the Commonwealth determined to restore the country to her old position. In particular he wanted to encourage English shipping and trade overseas. He, therefore, passed certain laws called Navigation Acts, which prevented goods being taken to or from English possessions except in English ships. This brought about a war with the Dutch who had most of the carrying trade in their hand, particularly that connected with India. There were some hard fought battles at sea between the English and Dutch fleets in which England produced a famous Admiral —Robert Blake. In the end the Dutch were beaten and most of their trade passed into the hands of the English.

Cromwell the Lord Protector.

In 1653 Cromwell had a serious quarrel with the remains of the Long Parliament and turned it out. He tried another Parliament but soon quarrelled with this also. Then, by what was called the Instrument of Government, Cromwell was made the ruler of England with the title of Lord Protector. From this time, till his death in 1658, Cromwell was practically King of England in all but name. He was a soldier and his rule was that of a soldier. When he failed to govern with the help of Parliament he governed with the help of his army. England was divided up into districts and each district was put under one of Cromwell's officers.

Cromwell's rule was a strong one. He made up his mind to make England feared on the Continent and he made an alliance with France against Spain. The Spaniards were beaten in several battles and the important island of Jamaica in the West Indies was taken from them in 1655, and has ever since been a British possession.

Cromwell tried to unite England, Scotland and Ireland more closely together and his Parliament included members from both Scotland and Ireland. But after his time the plan was given up and it was not till many years afterwards that the countries were really united together.

Death of Cromwell.

Parliament wished Cromwell to become king but he always refused to do this. He died on 3rd September 1658 and was succeeded as Lord Protector by his son Richard, just as though he had been a king. Cromwell was a very great man and England owes much to him. It is true that many people hated his religious policy and his military rule. Many men too could not forgive him for putting the King to death. But he restored order and he also restored the position of England as a European power.

On his death confusion followed. Richard Cromwell was a weak man, quite unfit to govern the country. Quarrels broke out between the army and the Parliament as, now that Oliver Cromwell was dead, the Parliament tried to take the power into its own hands again. All over the country men wished the King back again and Charles who was living in Holland issued a proclamation in which he promised to rule properly and to forgive all that had been done in the past. At last one of Cromwell's officers, General Monk, marched down with his army. Under his orders an altogether fresh Parliament was chosen. This was called a Convention as it was not a regular parliament, because it had not been called together by the King.

The Restoration.

This Convention voted that the King should be asked to come back and that the old system of government by King, Lords, and Commons should be restored. On 5th May 1660, Charles II was proclaimed King in London and on 29th May he entered the city amid great rejoicing, for everybody was glad to see him back again. This is known in history as the Restoration.

CHAPTER XII

The Restoration.

Charles II 1660—1685.

The nation was getting tired of the sad and serious Puritans, who had stopped sports and amusements of all kinds, and wanted some sort of change. The exiled Charles was therefore welcomed with open arms. For a time all was rejoicing, and Charles and his courtiers plunged at once into gaiety and merry-making, so that the King came to be known as the " Merry Monarch."

Character of Charles II.

If Charles had had the good of his people at heart, if he could, at times, rise above these pleasures, he might have been a great king. But he had no high aims. The sufferings of early years seemed to have taught him nothing but a wish to enjoy himself when king, and not to lose the crown which gave him the chance of this enjoyment. He never understood that there was such a thing as duty. It has been recorded of him,

> ' He never did a foolish thing,
> Nor ever did a wise one.'

Yet, if he was not capable of wise acts, he was, all the same, shrewd enough to see when not to do foolish ones. And it was this shrewdness that saved him from the fate of his father or that of his brother, which we shall soon learn.

He was not the sort of man to care much about religion. Before he came back, he had secretly acknowledged himself to be a Catholic and he confessed the same when he was dying. But during his reign he openly spoke of himself as a Protestant.

Reaction.

About a year after the King came back, a new Parliament was elected. So pleased were the people with the Restoration that they chiefly elected Cavaliers. The King and the new Parliament set to work to make things as they had been before the civil war. Cromwell's soldiers were sent back to their homes. Only three regiments were kept, and these regiments were the beginning of the present army. Some of the men who had sat in the Court which condemned Charles I were tried and executed. The bodies of Cromwell and two others were dug up and hanged. Cromwell's union of England with Scotland and Ireland was dissolved and Scotland and Ireland had again their own Parliament. The English Church was made what it had been before the Rebellion, and the prayer-book and bishops were restored. All men were required to belong to and worship in the Church of England. Those who would not go to the Church services were called Non-conformists (Dissenters) because they dissented or differed from the views of the English Church. They were punished for worshipping in their own way, and were not allowed to hold any public office.

There were brave men among them who were ready to suffer rather than do what they did not think to be right. One of these sufferers was John Bunyan who wrote the *Pilgrim's Progress* while he was confined in Bedford gaol for his religion.

The Great Plague, 1665.

In the spring of 1665, five years after Charles II became king, a terrible plague came upon London, largely brought about by the dirty and unhealthy conditions of the city. When people were taken ill of this plague, they nearly always died in a few hours after terrible sufferings. Every one, who could, fled from the city; but the greater part of the poor people were forced to stop and endure their fate. Shops were closed, traffic was stopped, and grass began to grow in the streets. A red cross marked the door of every house where there was sickness, and carts went round to fetch the bodies of those who had died. At the worst time ten thousand people died in a week in London, and it was found when at last the plague had ended that more than 100,000 persons had perished.

The Great Fire of London, 1666.

Next year (1666) another disaster befell the city. A fire broke out when a strong wind was blowing and quickly spread. The London ot that day was a place of narrow streets, where often the houses touched overhead. Many of the buildings were of wood and not a few had thatched roofs. It was impossible to put out the flames when once they had gained a good start. The fire lasted for three days and three nights and was only stopped by blowing up houses and so making gaps over which the flames could not pass. But about half the city had been burnt including the splendid Cathedral of St. Paul's. Great as was the suffering caused by the fire, it did good in the end; for it destroyed the old houses which kept air and sunshine out of the streets, so that the plague never came to London again.

Foreign Policy.

The principal interest of the early years of Charles' reign lay in his foreign relations. Charles renewed Cromwell's alliance with France and it was in pursuance of this policy that he married Catherine of Braganza, a princess of Portugal. Portugal was at this time quarrelling with Spain and was being helped by the French. Catherine brought Bombay as a part of her dowry, and this port was subsequently made over to the East India Company in 1668.

War with the Dutch.

Charles, however, did not maintain his independence as Cromwell had done, and before long, became a willing tool in the hands of Louis XIV, the King of France. Early in 1665 a war broke out between the Dutch and the English, as it had done during the Protectorate. The Dutch were defeated off Lowestoft. The English fleet captured New Amsterdam, a Dutch colony in America. The Dutch, at one time, sent their fleet up the Thames, sailed up the Medway, burnt three men-of-war and captured a fourth. At last peace was made. The

English obtained New Amsterdam which was named New York, in honour of the King's brother —James, the Duke of York.

The Cabal.

A strong feeling now arose among the commons in England against the King and his French alliance, for they had begun to feel jealous of the French power. What Charles wanted at this time was to become independent of Parliament and to get as much money as he could. Clarendon, who had been his chief minister since his return, was made to resign and was replaced by the Cabal, a group of five ministers—Clifford, Arlington. Buckingham, Ashley and Lauderdale,—(curiously enough their initials formed the word Cabal) who had little in common with one another, and were held together solely by the King. Immediately after making peace with the Dutch, he made another treaty with the Swedes and the Dutch known as the Triple Alliance, by which the three nations bound themselves to join together against France (1668) This was only to quiet down popular discontent, and to blind England to his real intentions. Not long afterwards he signed the Secret Treaty of Dover (1670) by which he agreed to join Louis in making war against the Dutch. Charles was also to declare himself a Roman Catholic, and Louis was to supply money and troops to enable Charles to do without Parliament. The treaty was to remain a secret; and only the two Catholic members of the Cabal—Clifford and Arlington—knew about it.

War against the Dutch.

Charles did not dare declare himself a Roman Catholic, but in 1672 he declared war against the Dutch and at the same time gave orders in England that the laws against the Catholics and the Dissenters should no longer be enforced. This order was known as the Declaration of Indulgence. In the struggle that followed, the English and the French 'did not win more glory than they deserved.' At sea they sustained defeats, on land their onset was checked by the Dutch, who cut the dykes and flooded large areas of the country.

The Test Act.

This state of affairs could not but arouse the suspicions of the people. They felt there was something arranged of which they were kept ignorant. A Protestant and friendly power had been attacked. James, Duke of York, the younger brother of the King and next heir to the throne, was an avowed Catholic. All these things served to confirm their misgivings. Early in 1673 Parliament met to disapprove of the Declaration of Indulgence. So fierce was the storm that Charles was forced to yield and to cancel the Declaration. Parliament saw its opportunity and passed a law called the Test Act, which required every person appointed to any office—civil or military—to belong to the Church of England and receive the Sacrament from a minister of the Church of England. All Nonconformists, Protestants and Catholics alike, were thus debarred from holding any office and continued to be so till early in the 19th century. The

King now gave way at all points. He was shrewd enough not to contend against forces too strong for him, for he did not wish, as he said, 'to set out on his travels again.' He married the princess Mary, elder daughter of the Duke of York, to William III of Orange, the chief ruler of the Dutch and the leading Protestant in Europe. The Test Act put an end to the Cabal. The two Catholic members had to resign. The third important member Ashley, who had lately been made the Earl of Shaftesbury, had already withdrawn as he felt he had been kept in the dark about the Secret Treaty.

The Popish Plot.

Just at this time when men were suspicious of the King, a story spread which threw the country into a fervour of excitement. Titus Oates, a clergyman of disreputable character, came forward and told how he had found out a Popish plot to kill Charles II and make the Duke of York king. His story was untrue but the feeling against Roman Catholics ran so high that the wildest statements were accepted. Oates was made a hero and many innocent Catholics were tried and put to death.

Whigs and Tories.

The Earl of Shaftesbury, though he had no part in Oates' appearance, endeavoured to profit by the situation and did everything to encourage a belief in the reality of the Popish plot. He declared himself to be the champion of Protestantism and succeeded to some extent in weakening the King's party. Just at this time Louis revenged himself for the marriage of Mary to William of Orange by giving out the fact that Charles had asked him for money to enable him to dispense with Parliament. This threw the Parliament into Shaftesbury's arms and he became the leader of a large majority. His followers were called the Whig party, those of the King the Tory party. The two names were at first given as nicknames. Whig is a Scotch word meaning sour milk and was first given in Scotland to some people in the west of the country who were then in revolt. Tory is an Irish word meaning robber. In course of time these names were accepted by the parties, and men felt proud of being Whigs and Tories. From this time begins the division of Parliament into parties.

The Habeas Corpus Act.

The Earl of Shaftesbury was anxious that the Duke of York should not succeed his brother, and in 1679 he brought forward an Exclusion Bill which was to disqualify him for the throne because he was a Roman Catholic. Between 1679 and 1681 three Short Parliaments were held in all, of which the Whigs were in a majority. The first Short Parliament passed a bill of great importance, the Habeas Corpus Act. One of the provisions of the Great Charter had been that 'no man shall be taken or imprisoned unless by lawful judgment of his peers or the law of the land.' Ever since the passing of the Charter, every Englishman who was put into prison, could, as a matter of right, apply for a writ of 'Habeas Corpus' (meaning 'produce the body'), which made it obligatory on the gaoler to produce his prisoner in court, and show the warrant indicating his crime. But judges and kings had managed to ignore these writs when it suited their convenience. The Earl of Shaftesbury now brought in a Habeas Corpus Act; its aim was to prevent a person from being put into prison without trial. The language was so clear that the law could not be misinterpreted. But the bill which Shaftesbury was anxious to get passed was the Exclusion Bill. The first Short Parliament was dissolved by the King before the bill could be passed. In the second the bill was again brought in. It was passed in the Commons but was rejected in the House of Lords. In the third the bill was once again discussed, but the King again dissolved Parliament and ruled without one until his death.

The Rye House Plot.

The King kept a very prudent attitude throughout this period. He was biding his time. He let Shaftesbury have his own way, but Shaftesbury was so violent in his ways, that he soon lost the sympathy of the people. The panic against the Papists was now gradually dying down. The falsehoods of Oates were coming to light. There was a strong Tory reaction. Public opinion had swung to the King's side and it was not uncommon now to hear of the 'divine right of kings' being preached. The Whigs, furious at the reaction against them, talked of appealing to arms, but with the bitter memories of the Civil War still fresh and terrible in men's minds, this proposal could not meet with popular support. In 1683 some reckless members of the

Whig party formed a plot to murder the King and the Duke of York at the Rye House on their return from Newmarket. This plot is known as the Rye House Plot. It was detected, and the plotters as well as others were executed amidst general applause. Shaftesbury in fear for his life fled with others to Holland where he shortly afterwards died.

Charles died very suddenly in February 1685. On his death-bed he acknowledged the authority of the Church of Rome. This news spread all over England and people realized that their suspicions had not been without foundation.

James II 1685—1688.

Charles was quietly succeeded by his brother James. At his accession everything seemed to be in his favour. James declared that he intended to uphold the rights of the English Church, though he meant to remain faithful to his own religion. A parliament which met was thoroughly loyal and granted him a large income for life. For a few months everything went on well.

Monmouth's Rebellion.

Yet the succession was not to go undisputed. After the fall of the Whigs in 1681, the Duke of Monmouth, natural son of Charles II, had fled with Shaftesbury. In 1685 he came over from Holland to dispute the succession with James. He landed at Lyme Regis and gathered about him a large army of rustics. At Taunton he declared himself king, but before he had proceeded any further he was met by the royal troops at Sedgemoor on July 6, 1685. His undrilled farmers were no match for the regular troops of the King and were badly defeated. He fled, but was captured, taken to London and executed. James was resolved not to show any mercy to the rebels. The Duke's followers were hunted down in all directions and were shot by hundreds by the notorious Colonel Kirke who was sent for this purpose. James also sent the Chief Judge Jefferys on a judicial tour to the scene of rebellion. Jeffreys was known to be a very 'brutal and foulmouthed judge.' The assizes that he held were known as the 'Bloody Assizes' for the brutality of the punishments inflicted and the cruelty of the manner in which sentence was given. The number of those who perished in the Bloody Assizes was 320, while 841 were transported to the West Indies to work hard under a burning sun.

Declaration of Indulgence.

James now felt secure, and was led to think that the aim of his life—the restoration of Catholicism—could easily be accomplished. He appointed some Catholic officers in the army and excused them from taking the oath required by the Test Act The Commons protested and demanded that the King should observe the law in future. James claimed for himself what he called a dispensing power, by which he had a right to dispense with the laws when he saw fit and a suspending power by which he could, for a time, stop any law being carried out. He got a declaration from the judges that both these powers were vested in him. Now he openly began to violate the Test Act and to appoint avowed Catholics to positions of all sorts in the army and in other branches of the service. Finally in 1687, James re-issued the Declaration of Indulgence, announcing that all his subjects, Dissenters as well as Catholics, were free to worship as they pleased and to hold offices without any kind of test. The King hoped thereby to gain the Dissenters to his side. For the moment he partially succeeded, but when in the following year, he once more issued the Declaration and ordered the clergy to read it to the people from their pulpits, the whole nation united against him. The first act of open opposition came from the bishops, seven of whom signed a petition to the King asking him not to force the clergy to act against their conscience. The King ordered that the seven bishops should be tried for having published a seditious libel. The trial was conducted amidst great excitement; the jury at last gave the verdict 'not guilty.'

The invitation to William of Orange.

Almost immediately before this trial a son was born to the King. The whole nation was startled at the news. People had tolerated his rule so far because they were sure that Mary, his elder daughter, who was a Protestant, would succeed him. Now it was certain that his son would be brought up as a Roman Catholic and there was no longer any chance of a Protestant succession. On the day of the acquittal of the bishops, some leading men of both the Whig and the Tory parties sent an invitation to Mary's husband, William of Orange, to come in arms and to drive out James. In

October 1688 William issued a Declaration giving his reasons for descending upon England, in which he reviewed the misconduct and misdeeds of James. He also stated that he was accepting the invitation sent to him, as he was the husband of the heiress to the throne. His purpose would be to secure the election of a free Parliament, by whose decision he would abide.

He landed at Torbay on November 5, 1688, and meeting little opposition, at once marched to London. After a little time men of rank began to join him, and James soon discovered that all was lost. He attempted to fly to France, but was captured and brought back. William was not at all anxious to keep him a prisoner. He was allowed to escape a second time to France, with the connivance of William, and took refuge with Louis. The bloodless revolution of 1688, rightly called the glorious revolution, was over.

Expansion of the Empire.

During the reigns of Charles II and James II the expansion of the English Colonies continued. Carolina (so called from Carolus—the Latin name for Charles) was founded in 1667. New York had been conquered from the Dutch. Pennsylvania was founded by William Penn in 1681. In the extreme north of America also English occupation had begun with the foundation of the Hudson's Bay Company in 1670.

CHAPTER XIII

William and Mary.

After the flight of James II the state of affairs was complicated for a time. Many of the Tories wanted William simply to act as Regent for James II. The extreme Whigs, on the other hand, advised William to claim the throne by right of conquest. There were others who maintained that as James had fled, Mary had, as his heir, become Queen. William, though he did not want to go against the wishes of the people, refused either to rule in another's name, or, as he said, to act as his wife's gentleman-usher. Mary also refused to accept the crown except as a joint sovereign with her husband.

William and Mary.

On William's invitation a convention was elected and assembled on January 22, 1689. It declared the throne of England vacant. After a good deal of discussion it was settled that William and Mary should be joint sovereigns. Before this, however, the Lords and Commons determined to define the powers of the King, for they wanted to make it impossible for any future king to act as James II had done. There was then drawn up the famous Declaration of Rights, in which, after denouncing James' unconstitutional deeds, it was declared "that the

Declaration of Rights.

King cannot suspend or dispense with the laws, nor raise money, nor keep a standing army without the consent of Parliament; that subjects may petition a king; that all elections of members must be free, and that there must be perfect freedom of speech in Parliament, which should be held frequently to redress grievances and strengthen the laws. That jurymen must be honestly chosen, and in trials for high treason must be freeholders; while excessive fines, and cruel, unusual punishments must not be inflicted. Lastly, that no Papist should ever again hold the crown of England."

It was also arranged that if William and Mary died without children, the throne should descend to Mary's younger sister, Anne. Another law passed at the same time was the Toleration Act which gave permission to Protestant Dissenters to worship in their own chapels. The Catholics, however, did not obtain the right to do the same.

William knew he would have to fight for his crown. His position in England was now pretty secure, but it was otherwise in Scotland. While the Scottish Parliament had declared for William, a nobleman called Viscount Dundee, who is also known as Graham of Claverhouse, declared for James. He gathered together an army of Highlanders and drew them up at the top of a steep ascent through the pass of Killiecrankie, one of the most beautiful passes in Scotland. William's troops under Mackay came panting up the hill. It was a hot summer day (July 27, 1689). For a time the forces lay firing at each other till the

Highlanders grew impatient. It was midday when Dundee gave the order for the advance. The Highlanders raised their national cry which echoed through the hills around. The answer was a feeble one. "We shall do it now," cried one of the Highlanders, "that is not the cry of men who are going to win." The Highlanders rushed on, cutting down the enemy with their broad swords. Mackay's soldiers turned and fled. The Highlanders had won the day. Dundee, however, fell at the moment of victory, and deprived of their leader, the rebel clans could not profit by the victory. The cause of James in Scotland was doomed.

The Massacre of Glencoe, 1692.

In 1691, a sum of £15,000 was to be given away among such of the Scottish clans as would lay down their arms and submit to William. December 31 was the last day by which the chiefs could make their submission. One of the heads of the Macdonald clan, Macdonald of Glencoe, was late in doing so. William's Secretary of State for Scotland was anxious to teach the clansmen a lesson and he asked William's leave to destroy the clan as a warning to others. William consented.

The Secretary carried out his plan in a very dastardly manner. He sent troops chosen from the Campbells, the hereditary foes of the Macdonalds of Glencoe. They came in the guise of friends and were very courteously received by the clans. They lived amongst them, ate at their tables, and laughed and played at cards with them. Early one morning when it was yet dark, the soldiers surrounded the huts of men who had shared their food and fireside, dragged them out of their beds and put them to the sword or shot them down as they attempted to fly. This brutal act, the Massacre of Glencoe as it is called, caused much indignation against William, but the clansmen gave little trouble for the next generation.

Siege of Londonderry.

The situation in Ireland was more serious. The majority of the Irish still looked upon James as King. Notwithstanding many English settlers, the mass of the people were Irish by birth and Catholic by religion. At first they had everything their own way and chased the English Protestants from their homes. James himself came to Ireland with foreign troops and besieged the walled town of Londonderry, where many of the English Protestants and the supporters of William III had taken refuge. The inhabitants stubbornly defended themselves for 105 days. They held out through long weeks of starvation in which they lived on the flesh of horses and dogs, and on handfuls of meal which were doled out with jealous care. At the end of that time, three vessels laden with provisions succeeded in breaking the boom which had been placed by the enemy across the river Foyle, on which the town stood, and as soon as these had reached the city, the besiegers sullenly retired—July 30, 1689.

In the meantime William himself crossed over

to Ireland and defeated James at the battle of the Boyne—July 1, 1690. James fled to France and after some more fighting the remainder of his army surrendered at Limerick. Most of them went over to France and entered the French service.

For many years after this the Protestants ruled in Ireland. There was a Parliament in Dublin, entirely in the hands of the Protestants, and from time to time they made laws which reduced the Catholics to a position of mere serfs.

War with Louis XIV.

Scotland and Ireland had been brought under control. The guiding motive of William's life, however, was opposition to France. For twenty years he had been doing his best to break down the power of Louis XIV of France. He had accepted England's invitation, because he hoped to use her strength against the French. Louis was helping James so persistently to regain the English throne that almost all Englishmen were ready to fight for William. For nine years William fought against the French King. He did not do very well and his wars in the Netherlands were one series of defeats. But William, who was always cool on the battlefield, had a wonderful power of rallying his forces after they had been beaten, and the French gained little but the name of victory from their successes. At sea he did better and won, in 1692, a complete victory over the French at the battle of La Hogue. At last, peace was made in 1697 at Ryswick. As one of the conditions, Louis XIV promised to recognize the new state of affairs in England.

National Debt. All these wars had an important result for England. They cost a great deal of money. Even the heavy taxes which Parliament granted did not suffice. Consequently it allowed the King to borrow money from any one who would lend it at interest. The interest had to be paid yearly till the loan was repaid. This was the beginning of the National Debt which has now grown to an enormous amount.

System of Party Government. Another thing that came into existence during William's reign, was the system of Party Government. After his return from the war in the Netherlands, William discovered that the House of Commons was a little out of temper, because he had not done well in the war. The chief ministers at this time were taken from both the Whig and Tory parties, and whichever party happened to be stronger grew troublesome when it did not approve what was done by the King's ministers. A way out of the difficulty was suggested to him. He might choose his ministers, the 'Cabinet' as they are called, from whichever party had a majority in the House of Commons. This system has continued ever since. If the ministers cannot persuade a majority of the members to vote with them, they resign; and the King calls upon some of the other party to take their place. This was the beginning of Party Government.

Queen Mary died of small-pox in 1694. The English had always loved her, so winning were her ways and so charming her manners. She had done much to smooth the work of government; while William was disliked for being reserved and unsociable. Now people looked upon him as more of a stranger than ever. It is significant that the years after her death were characterised by a number of plots in favour of James, Jacobite* plots as they were called. In 1695, William won a success against the French and gained a short-lived popularity. A Loyal Association was formed for his protection. But he was still far from being popular, and even the satisfactory peace (Peace of Ryswick in 1697) with which he finished his struggle against France, could not make him so. By this treaty Louis acknowledged William as King of England and Anne as his successor.

Act of Settlement.

William and Mary had no children. In 1701 died the Duke of Gloucester, the only surviving child of Princess Anne, and it was thought necessary to nominate Anne's successor. In June 1701, Parliament drew up the Act of Settlement. Princess Anne was to be the next sovereign, and if she died childless the crown was to descend to Sophia of Hanover, the Protestant grand-daughter of James I, and after her to her descendants.

In February 1702, William was riding at Hampton Court, when his horse stumbled over a mole hill. William fell and broke his collar bone. He did not want to die, for he felt that he had

*From the Latin word for James, which is Jacobus.

not finished the work he wanted to do. The War of the Spanish Succession of which we shall soon make a study, had begun by this time. 'Now that this great new prospect is opening before me, I do wish to stay here a little longer,' he said. But this was not to be. On March 8, William died. James had just died in France and Louis promised to support his son James III in spite of his promises to William at the treaty of Ryswick.

Character and Work of William.

We must think of William as a great man in history. True, he had failed to please the English. He was a cold, harsh, stern man and did not readily make friends. He had bad health and this made him petulant at times. But he had a purpose, and for that he worked with patience and perseverance. It was to bridle the ambition of Louis and thus keep up the balance of power. Before he died, he had raised England to a position which she had not enjoyed since the days of Cromwell.

QUEEN ANNE.

1702– 1714.

After William's death Anne came to the throne in accordance with the provisions of the Bill of Rights. She was sincerely religious and was in many ways a good and amiable woman, though rather weak in character. For a long time she was almost entirely under the influence of John Churchill and his wife, Sarah. They were made

Duke and Duchess of Marlborough at the coronation. Sarah had been her friend ever since Anne was a girl, and by her superior cleverness had made her do anything she wanted. Even after Anne had become Queen she and the Duchess called each other "Mrs. Morley" and "Mrs. Freeman" just to show there was not much difference of rank between them.

Anne had married George, Prince of Denmark, a man of no character or influence. The Queen bore fifteen children, one dying after another. The little Duke of Gloucester died in 1700 at the age of eleven and he was the longest lived of them all.

John Churchill had distinguished himself as an exceedingly brave soldier. He had put down Monmouth's rebellion and he had been William's best General in the Netherlands. William saw what a clever man he was and made him Earl of Marlborough. But he never trusted him, for Churchill used also to keep up a friendship with James II. Towards his end, William's attitude became more favourable for, at that time, he saw in Churchill the one man who could carry on the war against Louis XIV.

War of the Spanish Succession.

One of the great events of Queen Anne's reign is the War of the Spanish Succession. To understand this we must go back to the reign of William III, for the causes of this war lie in his reign. The Peace of Ryswick had not really put an end to hostilities between England and France. A fresh trouble an invalid and it was expected that he would soon die. He had no children. There were three candidates for the throne, one of whom was Philip, grandson of Louis XIV of France. William did not care much what their claims were, but he did not want a grandson of the King of France who was already so powerful to rule over the vast Spanish dominions. Louis was not anxious to go to war again and William succeeded by what are known as the First Partition Treaty and the Second Partition Treaty in arranging that Philip should inherit only a part of Charles' dominions.

When Charles of Spain died in 1700, it was found that he had left his kingdom undivided to the French Prince, Philip. Louis accepted the inheritance for his grandson and set aside the Partition Treaties. To William this came as a shock; all his life he had worked hard to prevent the French King from becoming too powerful and now it seemed to him, he had absolutely failed. He was anxious to make war on Louis, but the Tories had a majority in the House of Commons and they would not back him up. A Grand Alliance between England, Holland and Austria was signed in 1701. The Allies bound themselves to see that France and Spain should never be ruled by one and the same king. England, however, had no enthusiasm for the war. At last news arrived which roused England. In September 1701, James II died in France and Louis acknowledged his son as James III of England. At once all England was filled with anger, for they could not tolerate a French king dictating to them who should be their king. The whole country rallied enthusiastically to William, and resolved that Louis should pay the full penalty for his arrogance William found no difficulty now in providing for war. He summoned a new Parliament which voted men and money. Preparations went on apace, but the King was not destined to see the harvest for, as we have seen, he died of a fall from his horse on March 8, 1702 and Anne became Queen.

The Queen, as we have learnt, was entirely under the influence of the Duke of Marlborough who knew he could do what he liked. His great wish was to begin war against Louis as soon as possible and to show to the parties of the Grand Alliance that he was quite as eager for war as William had been. War was formally declared against France in May 1702. Marlborough was to be the Commander-in-chief of the English and Dutch land forces. Prince Eugene of Savoy, a brave soldier and a friend of Marlborough, was put in charge of the Austrian forces.

Battle of Blenheim.

Now it was not an easy thing to make several princes work together, for each wanted the maximum gain for his own country with the minimum of cost and trouble. Marlborough took some towns from the French, but on the whole, the war went well for Louis XIV, who felt so hopeful that he decided to send an army to take Vienna. Marlborough saw what the French meant to do. He was in the Netherlands with his army, but he boldly set off to march all the way to Bavaria to stop the French on their way to Vienna. There his English and Dutch armies joined the Austrian forces under Eugene. The combined army came up with the French forces near Blenheim on the Danube. (August 13, 1704). The French were utterly defeated. This disaster shattered their power in Germany. After this battle Marlborough won further great victories in the Netherlands, the chief of which were Ramillies (1706), Oudenarde (1708), and Malplaquet (1709).

All this time fighting was going on at sea. A few days before the battle of Blenheim, another event not less famous took place in Spain, where also the Allies were fighting. This was the capture of the rock of Gibraltar by Vice-Admiral Sir George Rooke. It has remained a British possession ever since and commands the entrance to the Mediterranean and the route to India.

Treaty of Utrecht, 1713.

The people, particularly the Tories, were now getting tired of the war and were anxious for peace. Marlborough had always been a Tory. But seeing that his old friends would not support him he had gone over to the other side. The Whigs commanded a majority for a time, but now arose a cry against the Whig ministry which the people thought was not justified in fighting other people's battle for such a long time. People said Marlborough was prolonging the war for his own glory. Queen Anne, too, wanted to get rid of the Duke for she had got tired of the overbearing ways of the Duchess. In 1710 a new election took place and the Tories got a majority. Marlborough was driven from office. The first thought of the new ministry was to make peace with France. In 1713 peace was made by the Treaty of Utrecht. Philip was to remain King of Spain. England got Gibraltar and several other colonies of France and Spain. France agreed to acknowledge Anne as the lawful Queen.

Union with Scotland, 1707.

But before all this took place, a great thing had happened at home. England and Scotland were united into one kingdom to be known as Great Britain. Since James I became King of England they had had the same king, but different parliaments. The union effected by Cromwell was based on force and did not last long. William III had wished to make the two kingdoms one, but died before he could do so. By an Act of Parliament known as the Act of Union (1707) the two kingdoms became one and had only one Parliament--the English and Scots still sit together in both the Houses at Westminster.

This enabled the Scots to send their goods across the Border free of duties and to trade with the colonies on equal terms with the English. Though at first the Union was not popular, it united the peoples of the two countries into one nation and the crosses of St. George and St. Andrews blended to form the Union Jack.

In 1714 the question of succession was raised. The Queen was in bad health and Sophia, Electress of Hanover, had died. Lord Bolingbroke, the leader of the new Tory party, was anxious to bring back the Pretender, as the son of James was called. But before he could do anything the Queen died. The Pretender moreover being a Roman Catholic had very little chance. George, son of the Electress Sophia, who was a Protestant, was proclaimed George I.

The reign of Anne is famous in English history for the number of great writers—both in prose and verse—who flourished at that time. Among the best known are Swift, the author of Gulliver's Travels, Addison who founded the Spectator, and Defoe, the author of Robinson Crusoe.

CHAPTER XIV

THE HANOVERIAN PERIOD

GEORGE I

1714—1727

George I was fifty-four years of age when he came to the throne. He was honest and well-meaning, but rather dull and uninteresting. He did not know a word of English—in fact, he was too old to learn new things; and cared more for his Electorate of Hanover than for England or her people. From what we have read of English history it must be clear that no sovereign could hope to be popular among the English who was not dignified in appearance and thoroughly English in speech, habits and outlook on life. In spite of all that William III did for England, he was so unpopular that he once threatened to leave England and go back to his Dutch subjects. George I could not, consequently, be a very popular king. The English people put up with him because he was a Protestant and his rival a Roman Catholic who would not, even for the sake of the English crown, be persuaded to change his faith. We have already seen that, in spite of the Act of Settlement 1701, Bolingbroke was in correspondence with James the

Pretender and it was only because Queen Anne died before his plans were matured that George I was able to ascend the throne without a struggle.

As it was, the Jacobites were not willing to sit idly by and let George I rule without an appeal to arms. They counted among their numbers all the Roman Catholics, almost all the Tory leaders and many of the Scots, not because the Scots had any grudge against George I, but because the Union of 1707 was not popular among them and they were willing to stir up trouble even without sufficient excuse. The King of France (Louis XIV), too, favoured the cause of James, partly because the Stuarts were Roman Catholics and partly because he hated England on account of his losses in the recent wars.

'The Fifteen.'

George I had been just a year on the throne, when in 1715 the Highlanders rose under the Earl of Mar and the English Jacobites under the Earl of Derwentwater and Mr. Forster. For the first few days the rebels were successful but the rising was ill-timed and ill-organized. On one and the same day November 13, 1715 two battles were fought, one at Preston where the Jacobites were defeated and the other at Sheriffmuir where each side claimed a victory. By the time the Pretender landed in Scotland (January 1716) all was over and he had to go back to France together with the Earl of Mar. Even if he had landed earlier it is doubtful if he would have had a chance of success. Louis XIV of France whose help would have been of material advantage to him had, in the meantime, died and been succeeded by a young boy of ten. Moreover, it was easy to collect an army of Highlanders but it was not easy to keep them together, for, after a few successes, they melted away. Lastly, James himself was not a good leader. He believed that 'he had been born under an unlucky star and would never come to his own again.' By March 1716 this rebellion, the 'Fifteen' as it is called in history, was a thing of the past. Forster escaped but the Earl of Derwentwater was executed. The Highlanders were partly disarmed.

The Prime Minister.

George I did not know English and his ministers did not know German. Besides, he took very little interest in English politics. One important result of this was that he ceased to attend the meetings of his cabinet and left everything to be managed by his ministers. At such meetings his place was taken by a minister who came to be called the Prime Minister, though the term did not come into use in official documents till 1878. No sovereign has, since his time, attended these meetings and thus the struggle between the King and the Parliament which began in the time of James I ended in a decisive victory for the latter. From this time forward the history of England is not so much the history of her Kings as the history of movements under the direction of her Prime Ministers. George II once said, "In England the Ministers are Kings."

The South Sea Company.

For some time past English trade had been increasing by leaps and bounds. In 1711 a company called the South Sea Company was formed with the object of trading with the South Seas or the Spanish Colonies of South America just as the East India Company had been formed with the object of trading with the East Indies. In 1720 the Directors of this Company offered to take over the National Debt, that is, they induced the people to exchange their Government Stocks for shares in this Company. Believing that the Government was connected with it, the people were anxious to buy these shares and soon the value of a share of £100 rose to £1,000. Following its example many other companies were started, some with the object of doing honest business but others merely to rob people of their money. One such company was started for importing Spanish donkeys into England, another for making a wheel which should have perpetual motion, still another for turning mercury into a solid metal. Yet people instead of laughing at such mad schemes readily subscribed to them and a great many sold all their estates to buy shares in these companies. The South Sea Company, in its own interest, had to expose some of these bogus companies; but the exposure brought about its own ruin. In the first place, it is evident that, when the value of a share of £100 has risen to £1,000, a dividend of 50 per cent. will come down to 5 per cent. As a matter of fact the Company paid a dividend of 7 per cent.

THE SOUTH SEA BUBBLE.

or 8 per cent. which meant only ·7 per cent. or ·8 per cent. for those who had paid £1,000 for a share. Besides, when a general panic sets in, people do not distinguish between a sound and an unsound concern. In 1913 when the Peoples' Bank of India, Limited, failed in the Punjab some of the people withdrew their money even from the Post Office Saving Bank! In England when these bogus companies failed, the shareholders of the South Sea Company, too, were as eager to sell their shares as they had been to buy them before. The value of a share fell as rapidly as it had risen, and thousands of people were ruined. One of the ministers died of the shock, another committed suicide. So the South Sea Bubble, as the Company came to be called, burst.

Robert Walpole.

In their rage the ruined people demanded the dismissal of the ministers who, they thought, were a party to this fraud. It has been the good fortune of England that at such critical moments a man appears who saves the situation. The man of the hour was Robert Walpole.

This man had already been a minister but having quarrelled with his colleagues had gone out of office. He was known to have a very good head for figures and the people believed that if anybody could save the country it was he. So, in 1721, Walpole became the head of the new ministry. He took measures so that the shareholders got one-third of their money back.

Robert Walpole was neither a scholar nor an orator, but he was a keen man of business who knew how to manage the House of Commons. He was the first Prime Minister, though he never called himself by that name. To keep himself in power, he employed only second-rate men as his colleagues and elbowed out all first-rate men. In fact, he loved power so much that, when he found that the nation pressed for a measure of which he did not approve, rather than resign, as is the usual practice, he would yield to popular clamour. His chief failing, however, was that he controlled the House of Commons by means of bribes. The members of the Parliament, in those days, were different from what they are now. Firstly, they were not truly representative of the people, as we shall see later on, secondly, they were self-seeking men who wanted jobs for themselves and their friends and relatives. Walpole believed that every man had his price and that he could, by paying it, keep the House of Commons in effective control. In those days the proceedings of the Parliament were not published and nobody knew how a member had voted. These corrupt practices were therefore prevalent to a degree which would not be tolerated to-day.

His policy.

It must, however, be said to the credit of Walpole that though he loved power for himself and would resort to questionable means to retain it, he used that power for the sole good of his country and took nothing for himself except his own salary. The following four features of his policy are worthy of mention.

(1) He sought to secure the Hanoverians on the throne, as he thought that his own fortunes were bound up with those of that house.

(2) He was anxious that all power should be transferred from the House of Lords to the House of Commons.

(3) He avoided changes, grand schemes, and new laws. His motto was, "Let sleeping dogs lie."

(4) He loved peace at home and abroad. He did not want to involve England in continental wars. In 1733 there was a war in Europe, called the War of the Polish Succession, and Walpole could say with pride that, though fifty thousand men had been killed in one year, not one of them was an Englishman.

GEORGE II

1727—1760

Walpole had been in power only for six years when George I died and was succeeded by his son, George II. George II, like his father, was a thorough German, but he could speak English fairly well and took more interest in English affairs than his father. He passionately loved his wife, Queen Caroline, and it was because of her great influence over him that he kept Walpole in office, though at first he did not like him personally.

Walpole loved power and did everything to keep the House of Commons under control, but, naturally, he had opponents. Those intelligent men whom he had turned out of office simply because he did not like to share his power with anyone who could not be friendly to him. Even among those whom he sought to win over by bribes, there were some who did not like him because he did not give them enough money. Besides, there were men who were opposed to him because he gained his object by bribery. Prominent among these were the "Boy Patriots" with Pitt, who afterwards became Prime Minister, at their head.

So long as his opponents were the members of the Parliament he did not mind it at all. But now came a time when he found that the whole nation was arrayed against him.

War of Jenkins' Ear, 1739.

The Peace of Utrecht (1713) permitted England to send one ship a year to trade with the Spanish Colonies of South America. This privilege was, however, abused by the English merchants. One ship would lie at anchor in the harbour, but many others hovered about in the distance. In the night, this ship in the harbour was filled again and again with goods from the other ships. Naturally, the Spaniards resented this and punished the English sailors whenever they fell into their hands. One sea captain, Jenkins, brought one of his ears wrapt up in cotton wool to the Parliament and declared that it had been cut off by the Spaniards who had also insulted his King and country.

"What did you do?" asked the members. "I commended my soul to God and my cause to my country," replied he. Many people disbelieve this story to this day and are of opinion that Jenkins lost his ears in the pillory in England but the opponents of Walpole took up his cause and stirred up the whole country. In these days a minister will resign when he finds that he has lost the confidence of the nation. But Walpole could no more part with power than a miser with money. Much against his will he declared war on Spain in 1739. When the Church bells rang he exclaimed, "They may ring the bells now, before long they will be wringing their hands."

The War of the Austrian Succession.

Now, Walpole neither liked warfare nor knew much about it. Consequently this war was not carried on with sufficient vigour. In December 1739 the English took Porto Bello near the Isthmus of Panama, but two years later they failed to take the neighbouring town of Carthagena. This war with Spain soon merged into a bigger war, called the War of the Austrian Succession, which involved many countries of Europe. The Emperor Charles VI of Austria had got the consent of these countries to a document, called the Pragmatic Sanction, by which he wanted to leave all his dominions to his daughter Maria Theresa. But as soon as he died (1740) Prussia, France, Spain and Bavaria wanted to share his territories among themselves. Prussia seized Silesia without even so much as a formal declaration of war.

England took the side of Austria.

In 1742 Walpole was openly blamed both for mismanaging the naval war with Spain and for not sending sufficient help to Maria Theresa. His chief supporter Queen Caroline had died in 1737 and now his followers also deserted him one by one. He was obliged to resign but was raised to the peerage as Earl of Orford and was granted an annual pension of £4,000. Thus we see, that the Parliament was now the strongest power in the country. Formerly, the only way to get rid of an unpopular minister was to impeach him. But now the loss of office was considered sufficient.

In the war George himself led his army to victory at Dettingen in 1743. It is said that his horse took fright and was taking him to the enemy's lines. With difficulty he controlled it and getting down said, " Now I am sure I shall not run away." This was the last battle in which an English King took the field. In 1745, however, the Duke of Cumberland, the second son of George, was defeated at Fontenoy in the Netherlands by the French, helped by a brigade of Irish Catholics.

Anglo-French Wars in India.

In India, the East India Companies of both England and France fought with each other in the Carnatic. At first Dupleix, the French Governor, induced the Nawab of the Carnatic not to permit the rival companies to fight, but when French help arrived, he took Madras. The English attacked Pondicherry but failed to take it.

The Young Pretender.

This war encouraged the Jacobites to make another attempt to recover the throne for the Pretender. The Hanoverians had been on the throne for thirty-one years and had considerably strengthened their position but the people of Scotland had not yet been reconciled to the Union, and though they cared little for the Popish Pretender they cared less for the Hanoverian George, especially on account of the ruinous war now going on. In July 1745 Charles Edward, the son of James, landed in Scotland. Unlike his father, he was handsome and dashing, and soon won the hearts of the simple Highlanders who affectionately called him Bonnie Prince Charlie. In September he marched upon Edinburgh whence he proclaimed his father King of Great Britain. In the same month he defeated an English army at Prestonpans and then invaded England. The English people looked on at his bare-footed Highlanders but did nothing for or against him. When he reached Derby he heard that an English army of thirty thousand men were preparing to attack him. Some people believe to this day that if he had only marched on to London he would have succeeded in driving out George II, at least for a time. But his advisers lost heart and, against his will, he gave orders for a retreat. At Falkirk an English army overtook him but was defeated. Now the Duke of Cumberland (who had been defeated at Fontenoy) took the command. In 1746 was fought the last battle on British soil, at Culloden Moor. In this Charles Edward (called the young Pretender by the English) was completely beaten and had to flee in disguise. A price of thirty thousand pounds was set upon his head but such was the affectionate regard in which he was held that, though many poor people knew of his whereabouts, not one betrayed him. It is also said that, for three weeks, he was with a band of robbers who concealed him from his pursuers and gave him the best of their food. Disguised as a servant of a lady Flora Macdonald, he at last reached the coast where a French ship that had been sent there on purpose took him to France. In history this rebellion is known as "the '45." It was a much more serious affair than "the '15" because the rebels had a real leader at their head. Some years later the young Pretender paid a secret visit to England but he found that his cause was now quite hopeless. As a result of this rebellion the Feudal System in the Highlands was broken up and the people were disarmed. But the Duke of Cumberland behaved with such brutality that he earned the nickname of the "Butcher."

The War of the Austrian Succession was brought to a close by the peace of Aix-la-Chapelle (1748) which restored all the conquests that had been made. Prussia, however, retained Silesia.

Reform of the Calendar.

In 1752 occurred an event which shows how ignorant the general run of Englishmen were in those days. From the days of Julius Cæsar the year had consisted of 365¼ days, that is, a day was added to February every fourth year. But the earth makes one revolution in a little less than 365¼ days, that is, the Calendar got a bit behind the actual year. In 1580 Pope Gregory XIII discovered the error, set it right, and introduced the New Style in the Catholic countries. England, however, did not adopt it because it had come from the Pope. By 1752 the difference had grown to 11 days; so, when the Parliament enacted that September 3, 1752 should be called September 14, 1752 there were riots, since the people thought the Government wanted to cheat them of their wages or 11 days of their lives. It was also decided that the new year should begin on January 1, instead of March 25, as heretofore. According to the New Style a year divisible by 4 consists of 366 days except a century year which must be divisible by 400 to be a leap year. Now the error amounts to a few seconds in a century. Russia and Greece are the only countries in Europe which have not adopted this New Style. In India there is a movement among the Hindus and the Parsis to reform their respective calendars.

After the peace of Aix-la-Chapelle France and England were at peace with each other in Europe for eight years, but in India and America their forces were fighting. In India, since the two East India Companies could not fight on their own account, they took the sides of the rival claimants to the thrones of Hyderabad and the Carnatic. This war went on with varying success till, in 1756, Dupleix was recalled in disgrace. At this time, Clive came into prominence by his heroic

LORD CLIVE

defence of Arcot.

The English and French in North America.

This irregular warfare came to an end in one country only to begin in another. In America both the English and the French had planted their colonies. At this time the English possessed 13 colonies along the seaboard to the east of the Alleghany mountains, and the French possessed what is now called the province of Quebec and some territory near the mouth of the Mississippi called Louisiana. Just as Dupleix sought to drive away the British and establish a French Empire in India; similarly, the Marquis de la Galissoniére, the French Governor of Canada, (1747—1749) sought to drive out the British from America. Just as the French had trained the Indian sepoys in India, similarly they used the American Indians in their war with the English in America. In the end, however, the French as a political power were driven out both from India and America.

In 1749 the Marquis de la Galissonniére sent one of his lieutenants to establish posts in the Ohio valley. He went down the river and took possession of the territory by fixing tin plates to the trees, inscribed with the royal arms of France. In 1753 the Marquis Duquesne, another French Governor, sent out an expedition which cut roads through the forests and built forts at important points. The English felt that the success of the French designs meant that they should be entirely wiped out of the continent of America or, at least, their colonies would not expand beyond the

Alleghany mountains. In 1754 an expedition was sent under George Washington (who afterwards became the first President of the United States of America) against the most important French post, Fort Duquesne, at the junction of the two branches of the Ohio. George Washington, was, however, taken prisoner though released shortly afterwards. In 1755 another expedition was sent under Major-General Braddock, but this time, too, the English were ambushed by the combined French and American Indian forces and had to retreat with terrible losses.

The Seven Years' War.

But now formal war had been declared between England and France called the "Seven Years' War." Ever since the peace of Aix-la-Chapelle in 1748, Maria Theresa had brooded over the loss of Silesia to Prussia. In 1756 France, Saxony, and Sweden joined her. To check the growing power of France, England took the side of Prussia.

This time, too, the war did not begin well. The French captured Minorca and Admiral Byng who was sent to recover it came back without striking a blow. He was, however, courtmartialled and shot in 1757 'to encourage the other captains as a Frenchman wittily said. The Duke of Cumberland was defeated by the French and forced to sign a convention at Closterzeven by which he allowed the French to occupy Hanover. In America, too, the French were victorious everywhere. In short it appeared as if the English would not only be driven out of America but would be invaded even in their own home in England. An English statesman at this time exclaimed, "We are no longer a nation."

At this crisis William Pitt appeared to save his country, just as Walpole had saved her thirty-seven years before. But the contrast between the two great statesmen was very great. Walpole was a peace minister whose chief care was to keep England free from continental wars; Pitt was a war minister whose high ambition was to extend the British Empire. Walpole used bribery to gain his ends; Pitt was one of the few statesmen of those days whose conduct was above reproach. Walpole was a matter-of-fact man of business; Pitt was an orator whose fiery speeches roused the people. "Be one people," he cried when he became joint minister with the Duke of Newcastle, "forget everything but the common welfare. I set you the example." As we have seen, Pitt and his 'Boy Patriots' had brought about the fall of Walpole in 1742. He had faith in himself and in the English nation. He is also reported to have said, "I know I can save this country, and I know that nobody else can." Soon after he came into power (1757) the tide of war turned. In India, the battle of Wandewash in 1760 and the fall of Pondicherry in 1761 completely crippled the French power. In Europe, the British defeated the French at Minden and Admiral Hawke destroyed the French fleet in Quiberon Bay, near Brest, in 1759. But, in Europe, Pitt did not pursue the war vigorously; his aim was to help Frederick

William Pitt.

of Prussia with money so that the English might be better able to fight the French in America.

In 1758 Fort Duquesne was taken and renamed Pittsburg. In 1759 was fought the most important battle of the whole campaign which finally crushed the French power in America. In September of that year General Wolfe led his men to the heights of Abraham which commanded the city of Quebec. Montcalm, the French General, saw that his only chance was to give battle. Both Wolfe and Montcalm were mortally wounded in the battle, but the final victory lay with the English. The joint memorial to Wolfe and Montcalm bears this inscription:—

> Their valour gave them a united death,
> History has given them a united fame,
> Posterity a united monument.

Peace of Paris, 1763.

The Peace of Paris (1763) brought the Seven Years' War to a close. By it England gained Canada, Florida and Minorca. Pondicherry was restored to the French, but only as a trading station. Independently of this war, Clive won the famous battle of Plassey in 1757 which laid the foundation of the British power in India.

GEORGE III

1760—1820

George III, his character.

While the Seven Years' War was still going on George II died in 1760. His son Frederick had died nine years earlier in 1751, so he was succeeded by his grandson George III. George III was a very different man from his grandfather and great-grandfather. They were both thorough Germans, to whom England was not a responsibility but a burden; he was English by birth and education and 'gloried in the name of Briton.' They left everything to their ministers; he was resolved to rule as well as reign His mother's constant maxim was "George, be a king," and his tutor, too, had impressed the same lesson on him. He did not, like the Stuarts, claim the 'divine right of kings' but he took such steps, that, for a time at least, he enjoyed that right. Circumstances also helped him. Since the days of Queen Anne England had been ruled by powerful Whig families who controlled more than half the members in the Parliament and who bought up the rest of the votes whenever they wanted to pass a bill. The Tories who had, by this time, given up all hope of the Stuarts' return to England could wreak their vengeance on the Whigs by helping the King to break their power. They could persuade the people that an absolute king was no worse than a few families wielding all the power.

George III tries to concentrate all power in his own hands.

George III set about his task in right earnest and employed all the tactics of Walpole to concentrate all power in his own hands. By bribes, by patronage, by setting minister against minister and party against party, he created a group in the Parliament called the 'King's friends' with whose help he got everything done whether the cabinet liked it or not.

If George III had been as wise as the Tudors, he might, indeed, have changed the history of England. But he was neither fortunate in the choice of ministers, nor skilful in the handling of affairs. The first ten years of his reign were spent in finding a minister who would consent to be a tool in his hands, and during this period he changed ministers as many as six times. At last he appointed Lord North who held office from 1770 to 1782.

Popular resentment.

The efforts of George III to restore personal rule were, quite naturally, resented by the nation. Wilkes, the editor of a newspaper, criticised his speech after the Peace of Paris (1763) so severely that the Secretary of State issued a general warrant for the arrest of the authors, printers and publishers on a charge of libel against the King. Wilkes who of course was arrested, gained his freedom under the Habeas Corpus Act and prosecuted the Government for arresting a member of the Parliament and for issuing a general warrant which did not give the names of the people to be arrested. In this he was successful but the Parliament prosecuted him for libel. Several riots broke out, the rioters shouting 'Wilkes and Liberty.' At the same time a large number of libels were published against the King and his mother and as many as 200 printers were prosecuted. Before his case was decided, Wilkes fled to France, and, when he returned in 1769, he was again elected a member of the Parliament. The Government, however, imprisoned him for the libel. Again there were riots in London. The mob compelled the people to illuminate their windows in honour of Wilkes' election. When Wilkes came out of the prison, the word 'Liberty' in letters three feet high blazed in front of the Mansion House.

Another paper published a series of letters over the signature of Junius in which violent attacks were made on all men in power. It is not definitely known who wrote those letters but it is generally believed that it was Sir Philip Francis (afterwards one of the members of the Council of Warren Hastings). The editor of this paper, too, was arrested, but the Jury that tried him found him guilty of printing and publishing only, not of libel. The support which Wilkes—a worthless man in private life—and this editor received from the people gives an idea of the extent of popular resentment against the King and his servile Parliament.

In temperate language Edmund Burke, a

brilliant orator of the time, criticised the policy of the King in his book "Thoughts on the Present Discontent." Even in the Parliament itself a resolution was passed by the Commons in 1780 that "the influence of the crown has increased, is increasing and ought to be diminished." The people scored another victory over the Government in that they secured the right of publishing the proceedings of the Parliament.

The American War.

In dealing with the colonies it was the obstinacy of the King that lost America to England though, in this respect, his ministers and the England people must share the responsibility with him.

The relations between the Colonies and Mother-Country.

In those days every European country believed that the colonies existed for the benefit of the mother-country, so laws were not infrequently passed which sacrificed the interests of the colonies to those of the mother-country. In England, also, laws were passed by which no goods could be sent from America to any foreign country and no goods could be sent from foreign countries to America without first passing through an English port or, at least, paying a heavy duty there.

The American People.

The American colonies were, however, founded by people who had left their country for conscience's sake and who were prepared to make any sacrifice for the sake of what they believed to be their inalienable rights. In later years they had received new settlers from other European countries, notably France (which sent Huguenots) and Germany. New York, as we already know, was predominantly Dutch. This mixed population, thousands of miles away, could not hold their connection with England very dear So long as there was the danger of their being swallowed up by the French colony of Canada, they kept quiet; now, when that danger was removed (1763), they loudly complained of the laws which hampered their trade. These laws, however, were not so oppressive in their actual working, since they required a strong and efficient police to enforce them. In fact, these laws were evaded to such an extent that France received useful supplies from America during the Seven Years' War. The English Government had so far taken so little interest in these colonists that they were allowed to develop their own nationality and their own form of Government—democracy. After the Seven Years' War the English Government thought that these trade regulations should be enforced and further, that the colonists should pay their share of the expenses of the Canadian War since it had mainly been fought on their behalf.

The Stamp Act.

So, in 1765, a Stamp Act was passed which required all legal documents in America to bear a stamp. The Americans who had so long been allowed to manage their own affairs resented this interference saying that since they had no representatives in the British Parliament, that body had no right to levy any taxes on them. They even went to the extent of boycotting all British goods. This cry of "No taxation without representation" was very little understood in England where the Parliament was not, strictly speaking, representative of the people and yet the people had been accustomed to pay taxes.

American Discontent.

Only Pitt, who had by this time become the Earl of Chatham, sympathised with their point of view, but on account of his bad health he was no longer an effective force in the country. As a result of strong agitation in America the Stamp Act was repealed, but next year a new Revenue Act was passed imposing duties on tea and several other articles imported into America. At this the agitation was renewed and even riots broke out.

The Attitude of the British.

Lord North who came into power in 1770 removed all these taxes except the one on tea. Now it was not the amount of the tax that the colonists objected to, but the right of the British Parliament to impose any taxes at all. George III, on his side, was determined to be master of America and in this he was supported by his Parliament and the people who thought that the colonies existed for their good. For some time nothing untoward happened though the colonists steadily refused to buy any tea. In this connection it should be remembered that England grows no tea and this tea was all imported by the East India Company. In 1773 Lord North passed an Act by which he allowed tea to pass on to America without paying any duties at the British ports, but the import duty at the American ports was continued. He hoped that the Americans would give up their boycott of tea, now that it had become cheaper. In this he was mistaken. The Americans were as determined as ever not to allow any tea to come into their country.

The 'Boston Tea Party'—its Consequences.

In December 1773 three ships laden with tea arrived at Boston. A band of Americans disguised as Red Indians leaped on board, forced open the chests, and threw the contents into the sea. This "Boston Tea Party" as it is called roused the indignation of the British Government who closed the port of Boston, annulled the charter of the colony of Massachussetts (of which Boston is the capital) and placed it under martial law. The Americans, on their side, raised volunteers and collected large stores of ammunition to assert their rights by force of arms, if necessary. All the colonies except Georgia sent their representatives to the first Continental Congress at Philadelphia where they expressed their sympathy with Massachussetts, and claimed their right of representation, self-taxation and local juries. This determined attitude of the colonists made the British Government revise their policy, and in 1775, Lord North proposed that any American colony that promised to support its own civil and military establishment should not be taxed by the British Government. But before this news reached America, hostilities had begun.

Hostilities begin.

The first engagement took place on April 19, 1775. The English Governor sent a force of 800 to destroy a store of ammunition belonging to the colonists at Concord. At Lexington they were met by a resolute band of farmers and mechanics. Though the English succeeded in destroying the store, they were repulsed with heavy loss. The colonists now chose George Washington (who had been captured at Fort Duquesne) as their leader. It is said of him that he was 'first in peace, first in war and first in the hearts of his countrymen.' Before he took over charge the English army won a victory at Bunker's Hill on June 17, 1775. This hill overlooks Boston and is of great strategic importance. The colonists occupied it and repulsed two attempts of the English army to dislodge them. The third time, however, they were driven out. This battle proved to the English that it would be a serious matter to subdue the Americans, so they hired German soldiers. Indignant at this, the colonists resolved to throw off the English yoke, but, before they took this fateful step they submitted a petition known as 'the Olive Branch' in which they expressed their loyalty and desire for reconciliation. When this petition met with no response from George III, they issued their Declaration of Independence on July 4, 1776, ending with the following words:

The Declaration of Independence.

'We, the representatives of the United States of America, in Congress assembled appealing to the Supreme Judge of the rectitude of our intentions solemnly publish and declare that these United Colonies are, and of right, ought to be, Free and Independent States.'

France joins America.

For some time the trained English soldiers were more than a match for the untrained American volunteers, but in 1777 the British army under General Burgoyne was forced to surrender at Saratoga. Even now it is doubtful whether the Americans would have come out successful in this struggle for freedom, but after this battle the French who had not forgotten their defeats in the Seven Years' War entered the arena on behalf of America. The Earl of Chatham had foreseen that France would join America. He had done as much as lay in his power to induce his countrymen to conciliate America, but he could not bear the thought of America cutting off all connection with the mother-country. Weak with age and ill-health he came down to the Parliament on April 7, 1778 to urge the members to bid defiance to their old enemy France and not to allow America to break away from England. But his speech was scarcely audible. The Duke of Richmond made a weak speech in reply. The Earl of Chatham rose again, but fell down in a swoon. He was carried home where he died on May 11, 1778.

Spain joins America.

In 1779 Spain joined France and laid siege to Gibraltar. These events turned the tide of the war. In 1781 a British army under Lord Cornwallis (who afterwards became a Governor-General in India) cut off by Washington by land and a French fleet by sea had to surrender at Yorktown. These disasters made Lord North very unpopular and he had to resign in 1782. His successors then began to arrange for peace. But France wanted Bengal and Spain claimed Gibraltar which the British were not prepared to cede. Fortunately, in 1782, Admiral Rodney inflicted a crushing defeat on the French Admiral de Grasse who was on his way to seize Jamaica in the West Indies.

The end of the War. The same year Lord Howe was sent to relieve Gibraltar which had been gallantly defended for three years and Spain was compelled to raise the siege. When peace was signed in 1783, America gained her independence, Spain, Florida and Minorca, and France nothing.

Indian affairs. This loss of America was more than compensated for by a gain on the other side of the world. In 1765 the year when the Stamp Act was passed the East India Company got the right to collect the revenues of the three provinces of Bengal, Behar and Orissa—as important a step in the building up of the British Empire in India as the Battle of Plassey The servants of the Company, however, grossly abused their powers. They not only cheated their Company by engaging in private trade, but they oppressed the people of India. In 1773 Lord North's Government passed a Regulating Act to control the affairs of the East India Company

WILLIAM PITT

Fox and Pitt.

It is unnecessary to name all the successors of Lord North but two of them deserve notice. The first was Fox. This man was a mixture of opposites; he severely criticised the policy of Lord North but accepted office with him in 1784. To the last he spoke in favour of the French revolutionists, yet joined the Ministry of All the Talents in 1805 to carry on war against them. He was heartily disliked by George III who kept him in office only so long as he could not help it. The second man was the younger Pitt, the second son of the Earl of Chatham. This man had been trained in politics from his schoolboy days and was not yet twenty-five when he became Prime Minister. He was not a man of extraordinary abilities, but he had a firm determination and people had implicit faith in him because he was the son of the Earl of Chatham. In fact, he was the only minister who could please both the King and the people and who, for a time, made the King popular. His threefold aim was to reduce the National Debt, to lighten the taxes and to make the Parliament more representative of the people. But an event happened which thwarted all his schemes.

Condition of England and France compared.

In England, the people had fought out their struggle with the Crown, the nobility and the Church. In 1215 they forced their King John to agree to the *Magna Charta*. In 1267 they got their Parliament. In 1649 they tried their King Charles I and put him to death. For a time they tried the experiment of a republic but had to restore monarchy. In 1688 they drove out their King James II and during the Hanoverian period the sovereigns ceased to attend the meetings of the Cabinet. The Crown and the nobility in their mutual struggles for power had weakened each other and increased the power and importance of the people. The Church too, in spite of the sacrifices of men like Thomas Becket, had finally to submit to the Crown and to declare Henry VIII as its Supreme Head. The Reformation had thrown off the Popish yoke. The people of France, on the other hand, had not yet emerged from the Middle Ages as far as Government was concerned. They had still to bow down to the threefold tyranny of the despotic King, the haughty nobility and the intolerant Church. In England, only the eldest son of a peer succeeds to his title, and all the other sons are commoners who mix freely with the common people, in France every son of a noble was considered a noble and thus the number of nobles enormously increased. In England all had to pay the same taxes, in France only the common people had to pay taxes from which the nobles and the clergy were exempt. Since the number of nobles, that is, those who were exempt from the payment of any taxes increased, the burden of taxation fell more and more heavily on the common people. Moreover, the nobles and the clergy who owned most of the land did not live on their estates but spent their time and money in Paris and thus were quite out of touch and out of sympathy with their tenants. The lot of the common people was very miserable, they had not a mill to grind their corn and not an oven to bake their bread. For the use of the mill and the oven they had to pay a heavy fee to their landlord. They had to pay a toll if they used a road, crossed a bridge or entered a town. These tolls discouraged trade. The game laws, too, told heavily on the poor people. Peasants were not allowed to fence their fields against the wild boar, deer and other destructive animals lest the nobles should be obstructed in their hunting This miserable state of affairs was one of the causes of the failure of the French in their struggle against the English both in India and America.

France ripe for a revolution.

Bad as was the condition of France, it was by no means so bad as that of some other countries of Europe. But what made matters worse was that, in one respect, France was the equal of England or any other country in the world. She had produced brilliant writers and thinkers like Diderot, Voltaire and Rousseau who roused the people to a sense of their situation. Education was very common among the middle classes who began boldly to ask, "Why should the common people alone pay all the taxes? Why should the nobles and the clergy be free? Why should there be a privileged and an unprivileged class?" So long as the French armies were victorious, as in the days of Louis XIV, the King could still command respect, but the defeats of the French in their recent wars with the English lowered the prestige of the crown. The establishment of the Independent Republic of America, too set an example of what the French might and ought to do.

Louis XVI succeeds to the French throne.

In 1774 Louis XVI succeeded to the throne of France. He was well-meaning but weak and very much in the hands of his wife. There had been some bad harvests and he was anxious to do everything to alleviate the misery of his people but his selfish nobles would not allow him to take any practical step.

The French had their Parliament called the Estates General, but its function was only to advise and petition the King. In England, we have seen that King Charles I tried to govern without a Parliament but had to summon one after ten years. In France, the kings were so independent of the people that, after 1614, the Estates General had not been called.

National Assembly.

In 1789 Louis XVI summoned the Estates General. This body soon converted itself into a National Assembly, curtailed the powers of the King and drew up a body of rules for the government of the country.

The French Revolution begins. Fall of the Bastille.

On July 14 of the same year a rumour spread that the Governor of the Bastille, the State prison in Paris, had been ordered to load his guns and direct them against the town. As happens on such occasions, the mob of Paris did not wait to verify the truth of the rumour, but stormed the building, set the prisoners at liberty and massacred the guard. The French Revolution had begun.

Attack on the royal palace.

There was again a famine, and again a rumour spread that the King had caused it by buying up all the grain in France. The mob of Paris, 20,000 strong, attacked the palace, slew the guard, and would have slain the King and the Queen had not the troops arrived in time to save them.

The King of France as a prisoner.

The mob thus driven out from the palace camped outside and refused to move unless the King and the Queen went out with them, saying " Where the King is, there the bread will be." The King had to submit to this demand. The procession that accompanied him to another palace in the city was a strange one. In the front came a body of women bearing aloft the heads of the slaughtered guard. Then came the troops with trains of artillery followed by pikemen and pikewomen. Last came the royal party surrounded and followed by a crowd of singing, shrieking and howling women. The King was practically a prisoner in the hands of the Paris mob. In 1791 he and his Queen tried to escapes from France, but they were captured and brought back prisoners to Paris.

The French King deposed.

The constitution drawn up by the National Assembly in 1789 broke down and in 1792 the King was deposed. France was declared a republic and all lands were taken away from the clergy and the nobility. The people of France, like the Bolsheviks of our own day, believed that the people of other countries were as cruelly oppressed as they themselves, so they preached their doctrines of 'Liberty, Equality and Fraternity' and issued an appeal to the nations of Europe 'to rise up against their governments and to receive the aid which France would give.'

Austria and Prussia declare war on France. The French King executed.

On his side, Louis XVI had appealed to the kings of Europe who, for their own safety, sympathised with him. In 1791 Austria and Prussia invaded France. Such was the enthusiasm of the revolutionists that though they had no experienced generals to lead them, they not only repulsed these attacks, but captured the Austrian Netherlands (Belgium) in 1792 where they established a republic. When it was discovered that Louis XVI was intriguing to recover his lost power he was tried and put to death in 1793. Nine months later his queen, Marie Antoinette, shared the same fate.

All successful revolutions run pretty nearly the same course. There are poets, philosophers and preachers who bring it home to the people that they are suffering from grievous wrongs. Poverty, famine or some other calamity drives them to desparation. All of a sudden they rise, carry everything before them, and destroy the old order. Then they are divided into two parties, the extremists who demand radical changes and the moderates who do not want to go too far. The men in power under the old order of things are, in the meantime, busy intriguing to regain their lost power. The moderate party sympathizes with some of their views. Naturally the extremists think that these men are betraying the cause of the revolution and take strong measures against all those whom they suspect of treachery to their cause. In Russia and Turkey in our own times many people have lost their lives in this way.

The Reign of Terror.

In France, after the execution of the King and the Queen, there was a Reign of Terror for about four years when everybody suspected everybody else and nearly 19,000 people were executed. During such a period of anarchy the common people get tired of their revolutionary ideas and long for peace. So they welcome a military dictator who, at least, establishes peace and order. In England such a man was Cromwell, in France it was Napoleon. In our own day, Lenin and Mustafa Kemal Pasha assumed supreme powers in Russia and Turkey, respectively.

The English attitude towards the revolutionists.

In the beginning the English people sympathized with the French. They believed that France was following in their own footsteps. When the news of the fall of the Bastille reached England, Fox is reported to have said: "How much it is the greatest event that ever happened in the world and how much the best!" Clubs were started in some parts of England to discuss and spread revolutionary principles. But when the Reign of Terror set in, many people changed their attitude. The Parliament in those days was controlled by the large landowners and the mercantile classes—people who are the last in the world to welcome any change that removes inequality among men. The general appeal of the revolutionists to the nations of Europe to rise against their governments alarmed Pitt. He laid aside his schemes for the reform of the Parliament, suspended the Habeas Corpus Act, forbade political meetings, imprisoned leaders of political clubs, and passed laws whereby undesirable foreigners might be expelled from England and uttering words against the King's authority was made punishable as a grave offence.

Pitt alarmed.

In Belgium which, as we have seen, the French captured in 1792, they wanted to make Antwerp their naval base. Now England cannot afford to see Belgium in the hands of a strong hostile power. It has been said that 'he who holds Antwerp holds a pistol at the heart of England.' The recent Great War was also brought on because Germany invaded Belgium whose neutrality England wanted to preserve.

Pitt held the navy in readiness but did not declare war. After the execution of Louis XVI, however, the French ambassador was ordered by the British Government to leave England and so the French declared war.

War with France.

For nine years England and France were at war with each other and other countries sometimes sided with the one, and sometimes with the other party. At one time England, Spain, Holland, Austria and Prussia formed a coalition against France. These allies were, however, unsuccessful. Though the

English were victorious at sea and on June 1, 1794, called 'the Glorious 1st of June,' Lord Howe the British admiral won a brilliant victory over the French near Brest, the French were everywhere victorious on land. They overran Italy and soon forced Holland, Spain and Prussia to desert the English and join them. This gave such advantage to the English that they were able to conquer the Dutch possessions of Ceylon, the Cape of Good Hope and Malacca and the Spanish possession of Trinidad. At this time Napoleon Bonaparte was rising to power in France.

Napoleon Bonaparte.

Napoleon Bonaparte was not a Frenchman at all. He was a native of Corsica, an Island that formerly belonged to Genoa but was sold to France in 1768 a year before Napoleon was born. The Corsicans were very indignant at this sale, because they felt that they had absolutely no chance of winning back their freedom. For this reason Napoleon continued to hate France for a long time. It was during the period of the Revolution that he got an appointment in the army, and after he had won some victories he made up his mind that, henceforth, he would fight for France and France alone. By sheer ability he rose to power till in 1798 he became the principal general of the French army. At this time Tippu Sultan was fighting the English in India. He declared himself a citizen of the French Republic and sought the help of France to expel the English

Napoleon went to Egypt with the object of pushing on to India. It was he who first conceived the plan of connecting the Red Sea with the Mediterranean by means of a canal, but his engineers wrongly reported to him that there was a difference of levels between the two seas, so the project was given up. Napoleon would have dealt a terrible blow to the power of England had he succeeded in his schemes, but at this crisis Nelson saved the situation.

Horatio Nelson.

Horatio Nelson, as a child, had given ample promise of his future greatness. While only three or four years of age he strayed away from home and when he was found his mother asked him: "Did not fear drive you home?" 'Fear,' said Nelson, "What is fear. I never saw it." Once, when he and his elder brother William were leaving for school after the Christmas vacation, they found that the road was very slippery on account of the ice. William was half inclined to stay at home and their father said, "Well boys, I trust to your honour, if you find the road impassable you may come back." More than once William proposed to go back but Horatio urged him on saying: "Remember, brother, our father has trusted to our honour." While still a boy he joined the navy and when he rose to be an officer he gave the following directions to the men under him: "Obey your superiors. Think every man your enemy who speaks ill of your King or country. Hate a Frenchman as you do the devil." "Frenchmen," he declared on

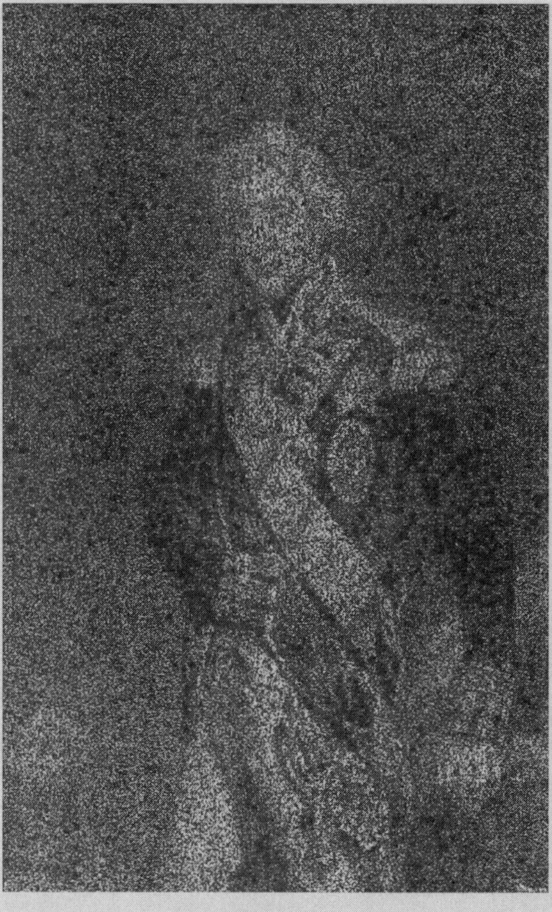

LORD NELSON

another occasion 'My blood boils at the name of a Frenchman." In 1797, when he was a captain, his admiral, Jervis, gained a victory over the Spanish fleet at the battle of St. Vincent and thus prevented a combination of the Spanish and French fleets for an invasion of England. In 1798 he was sent in pursuit of Napoleon. For two months he could find no trace of the French fleet till he found

The Battle of the Nile.

it anchored at Aboukir Bay, near the mouth of the Nile. Nelson put his ships between the French ships and the shore and thus destroyed them. It was during this battle of the Nile that a French ship—'The Orient'—blew up and the famous Casabianca, who would not leave his post without his father's word, perished. Napoleon was, now, cut off from France but he marched on to Syria, and laid siege to Acre. Here, too, he was defeated by the Turks helped by Sir Sidney Smith in 1799. The dreams of his

Napoleon becomes first Consul.

Eastern conquests were now shattered, and he hastened to France leaving his army in Egypt. Reaching France he placed the government of France under three consuls, himself becoming the first consul.

At this stage Irish affairs claim attention.

Irish affairs.

When George III came to the throne, the Irish had a Parliament of their own but only in name. All the laws passed by it had to receive the assent of the English Privy Council, and the British Parliament could pass any laws for Ireland without any reference to the Irish Parliament. When the American War of Independence was going on, the Irish leader, Grattan, thought it a capital opportunity to extort concessions from England. In 1780 all restrictions on Irish trade were removed, and in 1782 the Irish Parliament was made independent of the British Parliament. Still the Irish people, the majority of whom were Roman Catholics, were far from satisfied, because they could not become members of their own Parliament.

The Irish invite the French to invade Ireland.

In 1794 they invited the French to invade Ireland. The French readily accepted the invitation and set out on an expedition to invade Ireland in 1796. But, as in the case of the Invincible Armada in the reign of Elizabeth, a severe storm came to the rescue of England. The French transports were blown away and the landing never took place. In 1798, however, the Irish themselves rose in rebellion but were defeated at the battle of Vinegar Hill. This led Pitt to think of uniting the Irish Parliament with the British Parliament. By means of bribes and a promise to grant equal rights to the Roman Catholics he got the Act of Union passed by the Irish Parliament in 1800. But when the time came for the grant of equal rights to the Roman Catholics somebody pointed out to George III that he would break his Coronation oath if he permitted this. In the Coronation oath the British Sovereign had

The Irish Rebellion.

The Irish Act of Union.

to declare that he would maintain the Church of England. George III understood this to mean that to give privileges to the Roman Catholics would be harmful to the Church of England and so he refused to do so. Pitt was so sorry at his failure to fulfil his promise that he resigned in 1801, after being Prime Minister for 18 years, the longest period since Walpole.

In 1802 Napoleon was preparing for an invasion of England when his army in Egypt suffered a heavy defeat at the hands of the English in the Battle of Alexandria.

Peace of Amiens.

Both sides were now tired of the war and the Peace of Amiens was signed in 1802 by which the French gave up all their conquests in Italy and the English gave up all their conquests except Ceylon and Trinidad. The title of the 'King of France' which British sovereigns had held since the days of Edward III, was also given up.

The War revived.

This peace was, however, very short lived. Napoleon wanted breathing space and the English knew that he was busy making preparations for another war. He went on making conquests and hampering British trade and when the British remonstrated he called upon them to suppress all the newspapers that had criticised his policy and to give up all the members of the French Royal Family who had taken refuge in England. In 1803 when the English ambassador was insulted in Paris by Napoleon himself, war was declared. Napoleon was, at this time, at peace with all the countries of Europe and he made preparations for an invasion of England. England, however, could not be invaded except by the help of a fleet and the British fleet which was admittedly superior to that of France blockaded every French port. Napoleon, therefore, thought of this plan. His Toulon fleet should evade the English and join the Cadiz fleet. Both the fleets should then pretend to sail for the English possessions in the West Indies. While the English fleet was in pursuit of them, they should give it the slip and return to attack England. "Let us be masters of the English Channel for six hours," he said, "and we are masters of the world."

Napoleon's plans for an invasion of England.

The renewal of the war made it necessary that Pitt should again be at the helm of affairs in England. In 1804 he became Prime Minister and made vigorous preparations for the defence of his country. By subsidies he won over Austria and Russia to his side and formed another coalition against France.

Napoleon Emperor.

In 1804 Napoleon declared himself Emperor—a temptation that Cromwell had successfully resisted.

In 1805 Napoleon's naval plans were put to the test. Villeneuve, the French admiral at Toulon, managed to escape to Cadiz where he picked up that fleet and set off to the West Indies hotly pursued by Nelson. On his return voyage, however, his courage failed him, and, instead of entering the English Channel he turned southwards and entered

NAPOLEON ON THE BATTLEFIELD

Cadiz. Napoleon, infuriated at the failure of his plans, wrote him a very angry letter and himself set out eastwards to make up for the failure at sea by inflicting a crushing defeat on the Austrians. The admiral, on receipt of this letter, put out to sea to fight whomsoever he might meet and to show that he was no coward. Near Trafalgar he met the English fleet under Nelson on October 21, 1805, and here was fought the last naval battle of the war. Nelson hoisted his memorable signal "England expects every man, this day, to do his duty," before the action. The English gained a decisive victory though Nelson lost his life. Soon after, Napoleon crushed the armies of Austria and Russia at Austerlitz near Vienna. This victory of Napoleon weighed so heavily on Pitt that he died of the shock. "Roll up that map of Europe," he said, when he received the news, "it will not be wanted for ten years." After the death of Pitt, George III chose what is called the 'Ministry of all the Talents' because it included men from all parties. Among them was Fox who had been so ardent a supporter of the French Revolution. Fox prosecuted the war with as much zeal as Pitt, but he too followed him to the grave in 1806.

The Battle of Trafalgar.

The Battle of Austerlitz.

Death of Pitt.

Death of Fox.

The Berlin Decrees and the Order in Council.

Meanwhile Napoleon pursued his plans of striking at the 'Nation of Shop-keepers,' as he called the English, through their commerce. By the Berlin Decrees or the Continental System, as it is also called, he declared a blockade of all the English ports. England retaliated by an Order in Council declaring all French ports under blockade. In 1807 to make his system really continental, Napoleon defeated the Russians and concluded a treaty with them at Tilsit by which both the Emperors agreed that Napoleon should have a free hand in Europe and the Czar in Asia. It was this treaty that obliged Lord Minto in India to create a fourfold cordon against a possible Russian invasion. Embassies were sent to Teheran, Kabul and Lahore and the Cis-Sutlej States were taken under British protection.

The Treaty of Tilsit.

Napoleon appoints his brother King of Spain.

In 1808 Napoleon, as a result of some dispute in the Royal Family of Spain, made his own brother King of Spain. The Spaniards, indignant that a king should thus be forced upon them, rose in rebellion and asked the help of Britain. The British sent Sir John Moore and Sir Arthur Wellesley to Spain.

The Spanish resentment.

Sir John Moore had to retreat though, before his army embarked for England, he defeated the French at the Battle of Corunna (1809) where he lost his own life. Sir Arthur Wellesley was the brother of the

Marquis of Wellesley, the Governor-General in India, and had already won fame at the battles of Assaye and Argaum.

The Peninsular War.

From 1808 to 1814 he fought what is known in history as the Peninsular War. In spite of some reverses he won many victories and thus broke the spell of the invincibility of the French armies. The most famous of his victories were won at Talavera in 1809, at Salamanca in 1812 and at Vittoria in 1813 when he finally expelled the French from Spain. For these victories he was created Duke of Wellington.

The Peninsular War was such a drain upon France that Napoleon afterwards said: "The Spanish ulcer destroyed me." In 1812, Napoleon, at the head of 500,000 men, marched against Russia because the Czar had failed to observe the Berlin decrees.

The Retreat from Moscow.

On reaching Moscow he found that the Russians had deserted it. He stayed there for some time expecting that the Russians would come to sue for peace. But no Russians came and he had to give orders for retreat since the Russian winter was fast approaching. On its way back the French army was harassed by the Russians who had destroyed all the crops. Owing to the severe cold, starvation and attacks of the Russians, the French army lost heavily and out of 500,000 only some 60,000 invalids reached Germany in safety.

The abdication of Napoleon.

In 1813 Germany rose against Napoleon and drove him back into France. In 1814 Napoleon found that France herself was threatened with invasion. He abdicated and was sent to the small island of Elba, off the coast of Italy. Louis XVIII, the brother of Louis XVI, was made King of France. He was, however, not popular and, further, the allies quarrelled among themselves. This gave Napoleon his chance and he escaped from Elba and came to

The 100 days.

France where his old soldiers once more flocked to his standard. But he ruled only for a hundred days. The Powers of Europe were determined not to let him rule over France again.

The Battle of Waterloo.

On June 18, 1815 was fought the famous Battle of Waterloo near Brussels where the Duke of Wellington, with the help of the Prussian general Blucher, inflicted a crushing defeat on Napoleon. He tried to flee to America but he found every port guarded by the English fleet. Fearing that the Prussians would shoot him, he gave himself up to the English. He was exiled to St. Helena where he died in 1821.

Indian affairs.

While the British Government was engaged in its life and death struggle with Napoleon, Lord Wellesley was strengthening the foundations of the British Empire in India by his system of Subsidiary Alliances. Three years after the fall of Napoleon, the Marquis of Hastings finally crushed the Mahratta power.

DUKE OF WELLINGTON

Death of George III.

In 1810 George III who was subject to occasional fits of insanity went completely insane and remained so till his death in 1820. During this period his son George was Regent and on his father's death he ascended the throne as George IV.

George IV. 1820—1830.
William IV. 1830—1837.

The reigns of George IV and his brother William IV who succeeded him in 1830 and even the early years of the reign of Queen Victoria may be said to be a continuation of the reign of George III, for all the problems that demanded solution, or were partly solved, during these years had their beginnings in that reign.

The position of the Catholics in England.

The growth of the Party System in Government and general education threw the question of religion into the background, but still some fanatics opposed every law that sought to raise the Roman Catholics to a footing of equality with the Protestants. In 1778 the Parliament repealed an Act of 1700 which had placed heavy penalties on the Roman Catholics. When a similar bill was proposed for Scotland, there were serious riots and the measure was abandoned. Emboldened by the success of the Scottish rioters Lord George Gordon, a crazy headed fellow, led a mob of 60,000 to Westminster to present a petition for the repeal of this law. Since

Gordon Riots.

they were refused admission into the House, they broke out into an open riot. For six days the city of London was in the hands of the rioters who, with their cry of 'No Popery,' sacked the chapels and private houses of the Roman Catholics, burnt the Newgate prison, where they set the prisoners free, plundered the residences of the Lord Chief Justice and other magistrates and attacked the Bank of England. The rising was not put down till 500 of the rioters had fallen. Twenty of the ringleaders were hanged.

Catholic Emancipation Bill.

In 1823 a Dublin lawyer, named Daniel O'Connell, started an agitation to secure equal rights for the Roman Catholics—a pledge which the younger Pitt had not been able to redeem. At first the British Government tried to suppress the movement, but the agitation continued. In 1828 O'Connell and his party succeeded so far that the Test Act, which had for the last so many years been a dead letter, was formally repealed. The same year O'Connell was elected a member of Parliament by the County of Clare, though he was a Roman Catholic and for that reason ineligible for the seat. The Duke of Wellington who was at that time Prime Minister was not at all disposed to concede this demand of the Roman Catholics but he was quick enough to see that any further delay would involve the country in a civil war. So, in 1829, the Catholic Emancipation Bill was passed, and now the Roman Catholics enjoy the same rights as the Protestants in England.

Agricultural Revolution.

At the beginning of the reign of George III, agriculture was carried on as it was in the days of William the Conqueror. Most of the land was marshy, a great deal was left for the sheep and cattle to graze upon, and of the land that was actually under cultivation some part was left fallow so that it might regain its fertility. During the reign of George III marshes were drained, better implements were employed and by a system of scientific application of manure and rotation of crops, agriculture was considerably improved. Since these improvements cost money, the owners of small pieces of land could not compete with big landowners and had to sell their lands.

Inventions in Industry.

Up to 1765 industries were carried on in England as they chiefly are in India to-day by what is called the domestic system. Women spun wool during their leisure hours, and gave the yarn to the weaver who wove it in his own cottage where the trader came to buy it. In 1765 Hargreaves invented his Spinning Jenny by which a single spinner could spin a hundred threads at the same time. Shortly after, another machine was invented by which the spinning wheel was worked by water power. Close upon them came Crompton's Mule which combined the advantages of both, that is, it was worked with water and could spin many threads at a time. In 1769 James Watt improved the steam engine and in 1785

Dr. Cartwright invented his power loom which enabled a weaver to weave cloth much more quickly than before. Factories thus sprang up in the coal areas.

Improvement in the means of transport.

Side by side with these inventions the means of transport were also considerably improved. In 1758 Brindley made his first ship canal and in 1814 MacAdam, a blind Scotsman, introduced his system of making roads by spreading pieces of broken stones on the ground. George Stephenson, a collier, invented the locomotive engine and the first railway line was laid between Manchester and Liverpool in 1830.

The effects of the Industrial Revolution.

This change from the Domestic System to the Factory System is called the Industrial Revolution which though not bloody was very far reaching in its effects. Its one immediate good was that it brought wealth to England at a time when she needed it most, that is, during the Napoleonic wars. England could not only pay her own war expenses, but could help her allies with subsidies. England has, since then, maintained her position as one of the wealthiest and the greatest manufacturing countries of the world.

But this revolution brought many evils in its train. It brought wealth, but that wealth was unequally distributed. The rich men became richer and the poor men became poorer. The old artisans were thrown out of work because a factory did not always require so many skilful men to work in it.

The factory owners, in order to make larger profits, employed women and children of tender age and made them work for twelve or thirteen hours a day. The tired children sometimes went to sleep over their work and there were many accidents. Under the old system the artisan was a free agent. He worked when he liked, took a holiday when he chose and made his own bargains with the customers. Under the factory system he was at the mercy of the mill-owner who, since the number of the unemployed was large, could dictate his own terms to the workers. If the factory was stopped because enough material had been produced, the workers were thrown out of employment. Most of the worst evils of this system have since then been removed though some of the problems still remain to be solved. The old struggle between the King and the People has given place to a new struggle between Capital and Labour and at the present time has assumed world-wide proportions.

Parliamentary Reform.

For a long time it had been felt that the Parliament did not represent the people. Many changes had taken place since the time when the first Parliament met in 1295. Many flourishing towns had decayed and many new ones had grown up. The factory system was responsible for the growth of several large and important towns in the north whither many people from the south had migrated. Still all the places had to send the same number of representatives as in 1295. Thus one place, Ludgershall, had only one elector who proposed himself, voted for himself and sat as his own representative in Parliament. Another place—Old Sarum—was only a deserted mound with no inhabitants at all, yet it sent two members to the Parliament. Still another place, Gatton, sent two members to the Parliament but was only a ruined wall. These places were called 'Rotten Boroughs.' There were also what were called 'Pocket Boroughs' because all their votes were in the power of a single landlord. On the other hand, important and flourishing towns, like Manchester, Leeds, and Birmingham sent no representatives at all.

The younger Pitt actually brought in a Reform Bill but had to lay aside his plans on account of the French Revolution. From 1821 the question began to be discussed every year. It was not, however, till 1831 that the First Reform Bill, as it is called, was brought before the House of Commons and was rejected. The Parliament was then dissolved. Next year it met again, and again the Reform Bill was introduced. In the meantime the people cried for "the Bill, the whole Bill and nothing but the Bill." It was passed by the House of Commons but was rejected by the House of Lords. Riots broke out in many places and in Bristol the rioters were in control of the city for two days, until they were dispersed by troops. A third Bill was introduced and even now it was thrown out by the Lords. The excitement was intense. The King (William IV) was hooted and the Duke of Wellington who was the chief oppoment of the Bill was mobbed in London. The advocates of the Bill in Birmingham threatened to march on London 20,000 strong, and to compel the House of Lords to pass it. Now the only lawful course open to the supporters of the Bill was to persuade the King that the number of such supporters among the Lords should be increased. This could only be done by making a large number of peers from among the Commoners who supported the Bill. Lord Grey, the Prime Minister, advised the King to do this. This extreme step, however, was not resorted to, because the Duke of Wellington promised to withdraw his opposition, and when the Bill was introduced for the fourth time, he and a hundred other peers left their seats and so the Bill was passed. By this Bill, members were taken away from the rotten boroughs and given to the large and flourishing towns like Manchester or Birmingham. The rules as to who should vote were also made uniform. In towns those who occupied premises of the value of ten pounds a year and in the country those who held a permanent lease of land of the same value or paid an annual rent of fifty pounds got the right to vote.

It is interesting to note that all the Tories did not vote against the Bill. In fact, the distinction between the Tories and the Whigs as supporters and opponents of the power of the Crown had been abolished. Now these parties came to be known by their new names of Conservatives and Liberals.

Abolition of Slavery.

The new reformed Parliament at once justified its existence when the Bill for the Abolition of Slavery was brought in. The agitation against slavery was as old as the sixties of the 18th century. In 1772 the Lord Chief Justice had decided that a slave became free when he set foot on English soil. Still the carrying of slaves to the West Indies continued. The usual practice was this. Villages near the west coast of Africa were raided, often they were burnt, and much blood was shed before a sufficient number of negroes was captured. These poor wretches were chained and packed as closely as possible in the ships. Before they reached their destination, very many of them died and their bodies were thrown into the sea. In 1787 an association was formed for the abolition of slavery. Prominent among the members were Clarkson, Wilberforce and Zachary Macaulay, the father of the famous Lord Macaulay. The younger Pitt and Fox also sympathised with them. In spite of strenuous opposition both in and outside the Parliament this noble band carried on their agitation till, in 1807, they got a law passed by which the slave trade was abolished. It was not till 1833, however, that slavery itself was finally abolished in the British Empire. £20,000,000 was given to the owners of slaves as compensation and all slaves were set free. Since then the British Government has tried to get slavery abolished in all parts of the world. Slavery is now confined to a few semi-civilized and savage tracts of the world.

WILLIAM WILBERFORCE

Writers and Poets.

During this period England produced a great many writers and poets. Samuel Johnson compiled his first Dictionary of the English Language, and Sir Walter Scott wrote his well-known historical novels. Other famous writers and poets include Goldsmith, Byron, Keats, Shelley and Wordsworth.

CHAPTER XV

VICTORIA

1837—1901

Accession of the Queen.

William IV died in the early morning hours of June 20, 1837 at Windsor. Immediately after his death the Archbishop of Canterbury and the Lord Chamberlain left Windsor for Kensington Palace to communicate the news to the young Princess. After some delay the princess was aroused and informed of what had occurred. Soon she stood before them, " in her night-cap and her hair falling upon her shoulders, her feet in slippers, tears in her eyes, but perfectly collected and dignified." It was a great moment when the Archbishop and the Lord Chamberlain fell on their knees and saluted her as Queen. Her first words on being told of her new position were addressed to the Archbishop:

" I ask your prayers on my behalf," she said: and the two old men and the young Queen knelt together and asked God to give her strength and wisdom to acquit herself worthily.

As she was the only child of the Duke of Kent, fourth son of George III whose elder sons had left no heirs, it had long been known that she would succeed to the throne. She had been

QUEEN VICTORIA

educated with care by her widowed mother who had impressed upon her, from the age of twelve, the greatness of the post she might one day be called upon to fill. When the moment came, it found her fully prepared for the discharge of her onerous duties.

At first she depended a good deal on Lord Melbourne, the Prime Minister, for advice and guidance. Melbourne, hitherto an easy-going and good-natured man, now gave himself up entirely to the education of the young sovereign in her new duties. There was, however, the danger of the Queen being influenced by one party only. Luckily such a state of things was averted when Victoria married, in 1840, her cousin Prince Albert. The Queen found in her husband the best of friends and advisers. Educated like herself to be good and true, his sole aim in life was the happiness of the Queen and her country. He did not identify himself with any political party and devoted his attention to useful social reforms.

Early years.

The early years of Queen Victoria's reign saw many rapid advances. In 1837 the first electric telegraph was used on the Blackwall Railway. In 1838, steamships crossed from England to New York. In 1839 Mr. Hill, afterwards Sir Rowland Hill, brought forth his scheme for a penny postage all over the United Kingdom. Hitherto the payments for postage had been very high (a shilling or two being the ordinary charge which was paid by the recipient of the letter) and varied with distance

A penny post was now planned for the whole country and in 1840 anybody could send a letter, bearing an adhesive stamp, to any part of the British Isles for one penny.

The People's Charter.

The state of the country during these years of her reign was far from satisfactory. Ireland was not satisfied with Catholic Emancipation. O'Connell, the chief Irish leader, headed in the House of Commons a party called the Repealers who desired the repeal of the Act of Union of 1801. In England and Scotland, the condition of the working classes was deplorable. The Industrial Revolution had enriched the manufacturers, but had deprived many thousands of working people of the means of employment. Wages were kept low by competition, and the price of food was high. After the end of the war with France, Parliament had renewed the Corn Law, imposing a heavy duty on corn imported from abroad. As a result of this, the price of bread rose much beyond the means of the poor. It is recorded that children would often fight for scraps of food in the gutters and farm-labourers ate things meant for pigs. Naturally the poorer classes were, at this time, in a state of profound discontent. They found themselves to be no better off after the Reform Bill than they had been before it. Hence they set up an agitation for political power and there arose a party called the Chartists who drew up a petition known as the 'People's Charter.'

The chief demands of the Chartists were that every man should have a vote, that a fresh Parliament should be elected every year and that all voting should be by secret ballot. Since then many of these things have been conceded, but at that time it would have been unwise to grant any one of them. The working class still needed the political education without which political power is dangerous to those who exercise it. The Chartists kept on sending monster petitions to the Parliament. When these were rejected, riots broke out all over the country. In consequence of these outbreaks, the Government took measures to put down the Chartists' movement. The leaders were arrested and tried for treason. After 1840 the movement steadily lost ground. It was brought into prominence, however, in 1848 when revolutions were taking place all over Europe. It failed again, and died away in a short time having effected little, but having drawn attention to many grievances of the working classes. The Repealers too, like the Chartists, failed in getting things done their own way. Alongside O'Connell there had sprung up another party called 'The Young Ireland Party' who, unlike O'Connell, advocated physical force. In 1848 they made an attempt at revolt which was easily suppressed.

The Anti-Corn Law League.

Meanwhile more thoughtful men were discussing how to attack the real evil that lay at the root of their country's distress. They believed that the remedy lay in the abolition of the Corn Laws. Designed originally to protect the British agriculturists against low prices, they had made the price of bread almost prohibitive, and were believed by a large section of people at this time to be doing more harm than good. In 1838 an Anti-Corn Law League was formed in Manchester to urge the abolition of the duty on corn. The most prominent members of this association were Richard Cobden and John Bright through whose efforts the league soon became a power in the country. Of Cobden it has been said that he persuaded by convincing. He supplied all his friends with facts and figures to prove the wisdom of freely admitting foreign corn. Bright was more of an orator and impressed forcibly upon his hearers the injustice of making people pay a high price for the benefit of the landlords and the farmers. By pamphlets, lectures and speeches, the two men and their co-workers taught the public how adversely these Corn Laws affected the poor.

Sir Robert Peel.

The Liberal ministry under Melbourne proved too weak to grapple with this state of affairs. The Conservatives had a wise leader in Sir Robert Peel, a clear-headed and conscientious man who, though a Conservative, had an open mind for all practical reforms. They profited by the mistakes of their opponents and were able to drive them from power in the elections of 1841.

Peel's financial policy.

Peel now became Prime Minister, and in his new capacity, proved his greatness as a financier. Money affairs left by the Melbourne ministry in a state of chaos were set right. Peel had assumed office pledged to Protection, *i.e.* to protect* English-grown and English-made articles from being undersold in England by foreign goods, but experience was gradually converting him to the policy of Free Trade, *i.e.* of allowing all kinds of goods to come freely into the country. Accordingly, he reformed the tariff, and removed the duties off a host of imported articles, but the duty on corn continued. Cobden, who was at this time a member of Peel's party, had convinced his leader of the justice of his cause, but the landlords who still formed the larger section of the Conservative party would not lend their support. Peel was therefore powerless.

The Repeal of the Corn Laws.

In 1845 something happened which made Peel more determined. The potato-crop in Ireland failed and thousands of Irish people were plunged into fearful distress. Despite magnificent efforts to grapple with the famine, people died in large numbers and when the famine ceased it was found that, out of a population of 10 millions, 8 millions were left. 'Famine against which Cobden had warred now joined him as an ally.'

Peel felt convinced that the time had come to abandon Protection. He now saw that if the starving millions were to be fed, corn must be cheapened and that the only way of cheapening it was to take off the duty. Accordingly, early in

*This is done by imposing a special or heavy duty on foreign goods when they are brought into English ports.

1846, he introduced his Bill for the repeal of the Corn Laws. He was strenuously opposed by the larger section of his own party, led by Benjamin Disraeli, an ambitious, clever Jew, hitherto noted for novels, his eccentric clothes and for the brilliance of his speeches in the House of Commons. But Peel succeeded with the aid of the Liberals in carrying the Bill which enacted that the duty on corn should be gradually diminished until 1849, when it should be entirely abolished. This, of course, led to a split in the Conservative party which fell into two sections—known as the Protectionists and the Peelites. Soon after the repeal of the Corn Laws, the Protectionists joined with the Liberals. Peel had to resign and the Liberals took office with Lord John Russell as Premier.

Peel did not survive his fall from power very long and died suddenly in 1850 as the result of a fall from his horse. He was one of England's best and wisest statesmen, ever open to conviction, clear-headed in judgment and straightforward in action. After he left office, his followers long worked together under the name of Peelites. The most noted among them was William Ewart Gladstone, an able financier like Peel and a powerful debater.

Coalition Ministry of 1852.

After the repeal of the Corn Laws, and the breakdown of the Repealers and the Chartists, England settled down under the Liberals to enjoy a peaceful time. The Foreign Secretary under the Liberal Government since 1832 had been Lord Palmerston, an energetic and self-reliant man, having little enthusiasm for reforms at home but ever ready to take an active interest in Liberal movements abroad. Dissensions between Russell and Palmerston led to a division among the Liberals. Early in 1852, Russell was forced to resign and the Protectionists took office. Disraeli, now that he was in power, did not try to bring back Protection, for he knew well that the feeling of the country was in favour of free trade. In spite of this change of front, the Protectionists did not remain in power long. The Liberals patched up their quarrel and formed a Coalition Ministry with the Peelites. Lord Palmerston became Secretary for Home Affairs—a work for which he had no liking—and Gladstone became Chancellor of the Exchequer, in which capacity he drew up such brilliant free-trade budgets that he soon made a name for himself.

The Crimean War.

The Coalition Ministry was no sooner in office than the foreign affairs took a serious turn. Russia had been growing very powerful under the Tzar Nicholas, who regarded his neighbour Turkey with a jealous eye, and wanted Constantinople for his own. In 1852 a quarrel arose between the two countries about the Holy Places at Jerusalem and about the ill-treatment of their Christian subjects by the Turks. This provided an excuse for going to war and Nicholas launched his troops into Turkish territory. Turkey was weak, 'a sick man' as the Tzar had called him, and was no match for the mighty power of Russia. Fearing lest Russia should grow all powerful by seizing upon Turkey, England declared war against Russia in February 1854. She had as her ally, Napoleon III, a nephew of the great Napoleon, who had absolutely no motive in joining the war except to show to the world that France was a power to be reckoned with.

The fighting took place chiefly in the Crimea—a Russian province jutting out into the Black Sea. It contained the strong fortress of Sebastopol—the great arsenal of Russia in the south. If this could be taken, the allies thought that Russia would be forced to sue for peace. Unnecessary delays on their part, however, gave time to the Russians, and what had been intended to be the work of a few days turned out to be a protracted siege. The allies established themselves at the port of Balaclava whence they kept on making unsuccessful attacks upon the fortress. In their turn they were attacked by an overwhelming body of Russians. It was in this fight that took place the ever-memorable charge of the Light Brigade. An order was given to a body of six hundred and seven men to attack the guns of the enemy. Everyman in the brigade knew that 'some one had blundered,' but 'theirs not to reason why, theirs but to do and die,' and the heroic band rode for more than a mile through a torrent of shot and shell. Very few escaped and a French general who was looking on said: 'It is magnificent, but it is not war.'

Less than a fortnight later, the Russians made another desperate attack at Inkerman, under cover of fog The battle was won by the allies with the courage of their soldiers rather than the skill of their generals.

The siege of Sebastopol dragged on. But by this year the hard Crimean winter, this time unusually severe, had set in and the troops of the allies, unaccustomed to such cold, suffered dreadful hardships. Matters were made worse by gross mismanagement at home. It is recorded that a large stock of boots sent for the troops turned out to be all for the left foot. Disease appeared and under these conditions it was little wonder that the soldiers died by thousands. In fact, at one time more than half the army was in the hospital at Scutari near Constantinople. Miss Florence Nightingale with a band of trained nurses hurried to Scutari, and by her untiring energy, produced a complete change among the sick and the wounded. Many valuable lives were saved through her gentle and skilful care. When the miseries of the army were reported in Britain, public indignation drove the Premier and the War Minister from office. Lord Palmerston then became Prime Minister and began to conduct the war with his characteristic vigour.

Arrangements for the army were brought into order and the condition of the troops began to improve. The siege was now carried on more vigorously. On 8th September 1855, the Russians retired from Sebastopol and the war came to a close. In March 1856, the Treaty of Paris was signed. By it Russia agreed not to re-fortify

Sebastopol and not to maintain a war-fleet in the Black Sea. The Sultan of Turkey promised to place his Christian subjects on a footing of equality with the Muslims. This agreement, though satisfactory for the moment, did not prove to be a final solution of the problem of Turkey or of the Eastern Question, as it is called.

The Indian Mutiny.

For a few months Britain was at peace, and then a trouble worse than the Crimean War befell the British in India. Discontent had been simmering throughout India for a long time. Many things happened about this time that brought this discontent to a head. The belief among the Indians that an Englishman cannot be beaten, dating from the time of Arcot and Plassey, had lately been shaken by the Afghan disaster and the brave front put up by the Sikhs. British losses in the Crimea had been magnified and the British power was believed to be on the wane. What set the flame ablaze was the rumour that the cartridges which had lately been distributed among the Indian Sepoys were greased with a mixture of cow's fat and hog's lard. The outbreak commenced on 10th May 1857, at Meerut where the Sepoys killed all the English people they could lay their hands upon, and marched toward Delhi which was soon seized. In a few days half the North of India was in rebellion. At Cawnpore, a cruel massacre of women and children took place by orders of a rebel leader called the Nana Sahib. Lucknow was also besieged by the rebels but held out gallantly.

Fortunately the revolt had not spread all over India. The Gurkhas of Nepal were loyal as were the Sikhs and many of the Indian princes. Delhi was recaptured after a siege of three months and the garrison at Lucknow was relieved. By the spring of 1858, the last embers of the rebellion had disappeared. In the same year the rule of the East India Company was abolished and India was brought completely under the control of the crown. The transfer was announced on 1st November 1858 by the well-known Queen's Proclamation (the Queen was responsible for a good deal of its drafting) which is believed to be a Charter of Liberty by many Indians. Among many other things it stated the following:—

"......We declare it to be our Royal will and pleasure that none be in anywise favoured, none molested or disquieted, by reason of their religious faith or observances, but that all shall alike enjoy the equal and impartial protection of the law...... And it is our further will that, so far as may be, our subjects, of whatever race or creed, be freely and impartially admitted to offices in our service the duties of which they may be qualified by their education, ability and integrity duly to discharge..........

It is our earnest desire to stimulate the peaceful industry of India, to promote works of public utility and improvement, and to administer the government for the benefit of all our subjects resident therein. In their prosperity will be our strength, in their contentment our security, and in their gratitude our best reward......"

Some years later the Queen assumed the title of Empress of India (January 1, 1877).

The Second Reform Bill, 1867.

Palmerston died in 1865. As long as he was alive Gladstone had found it difficult to carry the reforms he had at heart. After his death, though Lord John Russell was the Prime Minister, Gladstone was the real chief of the Liberal Party He had changed bit by bit and was now an advanced Liberal. In 1866 he introduced a new Reform Bill. There were some members of his party, however, who wanted no more Parliamentary reform and his Bill was defeated. He had to retire from office, and the power passed into the hands of the Conservatives. Oddly enough Disraeli now brought in his own Reform Bill. Though a Conservative, he saw that it would not do to simply oppose everything and thus be a set-back on all progress, and he had gradually educated his party, so to speak, into doing those very things which they had once denounced. The Bill was successfully passed into law in 1867 and was one of Disraeli's greatest triumphs. It gave votes to all male householders living in the boroughs and in the counties to all who paid £12 a year in rent. This measure admitted the artisan class to political power.

Gladstone's First Ministry, 1868—1874.

The next election in 1868 proved adverse to the Conservatives. Gladstone became Prime Minister and remained in office for six years during which

WILLIAM EWART GLADSTONE

period he made good progress with his schemes. Ireland was as discontented as ever and Gladstone was eager to remove her grievances. The Irish, most of whom were Roman Catholics, were required by law to pay for the support of the Protestant clergy who formed the so-called Irish Church. Gladstone introduced a Bill which became law in 1869, by which the Protestant Church was deprived of much of its property, and its connection with the State was severed. The Catholics were thus placed on a footing of equality with the Protestants. This is known as the Disestablishment and the Disendowment of the Irish Church. In 1870 was passed the first Irish Land Act, the object of which was to give the tenants a better hold on their land and to make them more independent of their landlords. In spite of all this the Irish still complained that enough had not been done and the Irish troubles, as we shall soon see, were not yet over. In the same year, Gladstone passed the Elementary Education Act by which for the first time all children were compelled to go to school. The Ballot Act of 1872 was another reform which made all voting secret. Voters could now record their votes without the fear of other people knowing for whom they had voted.

There was a great war between France and Germany in 1870 and 1871. Gladstone did not allow England to be disturbed by what was taking place on the continent, and observed an attitude of complete neutrality towards the contending powers. People who were already getting tired of his many reforms at home now became dissatisfied with what they believed to be the tameness of his foreign policy. He was beaten in the elections of 1874. The Conservatives obtained a majority and Disraeli became Prime Minister.

CHAPTER XVI

VICTORIA—*(continued)*.

Disraeli's Ministry, 1874—1880.

Disraeli held office for six years. This period was marked not so much by reforms at home as by activity in foreign affairs and Disraeli did much to make England's power felt abroad. In 1875 there was a renewal of the old Eastern question. The Christian subjects of the Sultan broke out into revolt against the misrule of their Turkish masters. A rising in Bulgaria was crushed by the Turks with a strong hand. The 'Bulgarian atrocities' aroused the horror of the whole Christian world. The attempts of the continental powers to intervene jointly failed, and the Tzar. impatient of delays, took up arms for the Christians. The Turks put up a valiant struggle, but were defeated and made peace with Russia. Disraeli, who had now become the Earl of Beaconsfield, thought the terms of peace to be hostile to British interests and demanded that the treaty should be submitted to a European conference. A congress was held at Berlin in 1878, Disraeli attending on behalf of Great Britain. Certain districts of the Turkish Empire were created independent states, while others were allowed to remain in Turkish hands. Disraeli was proud that he had brought

England 'peace with honour This Treaty of Berlin failed like the Treaty of Paris to solve the Eastern question. A few years later fresh troubles arose which proved that the problem had not been finally settled.

After this there were wars in Afghanistan and Zululand. Though finally successful, the English suffered disasters at Maiwand in Afghanistan and at Isandhlwana in Zululand. Gladstone came out of his retirement to denounce Disraeli for his alliance with the Turks and for his mismanagement of these wars which were the results of his mistaken policy. Gladstone's exertions had their effect. In the elections of 1880, the Conservatives were decisively beaten. Beaconsfield resigned and Gladstone took his place.

Beaconsfield died next year, followed by the grief of the Queen, the sorrow of the people and the mournful tears of the party he had led. Handicapped by many disadvantages not the least of which was that he was an alien by race, he had raised himself by patient efforts to be one of the foremost men in England. He was not at first popular in Parliament and his first speech was a failure. But before he sat down he declared that the time would come when he would be heard. And the time did come. He lived to be not only the foremost man in the ranks of the Conservative party but Prime Minister. For years he was the one man in England, and one could say about him in the words of Bismark 'Disraeli is England.' He was a statesman of wide and imperial outlook.

Gladstone inherited from the Conservatives a number of problems with which by nature he was ill-fitted to cope.

Gladstone's second Ministry, 1880—1885.

Beginnings of Trouble in S. Africa.

The first European settlers in South Africa had been the Dutch who came to be known as the Boers which in the Dutch language means farmers. When Cape Colony (now called the Cape of Good Hope) came into the hands of Great Britain, early in the nineteenth century, the Boers migrated to the Transvaal, a district lying north of the River Vaal, where they set up a republic. But they managed their affairs so badly that Britain annexed the Transvaal in 1877. The Boers resented this annexation, and four years later, rose in revolt against the British. In this war they inflicted a heavy defeat on the English at Majuba Hill. Gladstone then made peace with them and restored to them their independence.

Egypt.

No sooner was this trouble over than the attention of the Government was called to the state of affairs in Egypt. Egypt had become very important to England since the opening of the Suez Canal in 1869. Under the extravagant rule of the Khedive, the country had been reduced to the verge of bankruptcy, when in 1875, the British Government, at Disraeli's suggestion, bought the Khedive's shares in the Suez Canal for four millions sterling. France was also a large shareholder in the Canal, and in 1879, the two countries jointly assumed the task of controlling Egypt. Two years later a National Party under Arabi Pasha arose to put an end to this 'Dual control.' The French refusing to co-operate, the British were left alone to deal with the rebels. Arabi was defeated in 1882 and Britain assumed the Protectorate of Egypt.

The Sudan.

In the meantime, trouble had arisen in the region on the Upper Nile known as the Sudan—a dependency of Egypt. Led by a religious fanatic who called himself the Mahdi, the Sudanese rose in revolt in 1883. An army sent against him was completely routed. The British Government then sent General Gordon, a brave English officer, to rescue the Egyptian garrisons in the Sudan. He reached Khartum where he was shut in by the Mahdi's troops, captured and slain (1885). The country was divided into electoral districts, roughly equal it was re-conquered by Lord Kitchener and has since been ruled by the British.

Third Reform Bill, 1884.

Though hampered by these troubles in South Africa and Egypt, Gladstone did not fail to carry out the internal reforms for which he was pre-eminently fitted. In 1884 a third Reform Bill was introduced and passed, by which the franchise, *i.e.*, the right to vote, was extended to all householders in the countries on the same conditions as those on which it had been conferred by the Second Reform Act on the boroughs. At the same time the country was abandoned to the Mahdi. Thirteen years later in population, each empowered to return one member to Parliament. The Act gave the vote to the agricultural labourers and was thus a further move in the direction of democracy *i.e.* government by the people.

First Home Rulers.

The more urgent problem, however, was that of Ireland. Gladstone's measure during his first ministry had not settled the Irish question. There arose further disputes between the landlords and the tenants, who were unable to pay their rent. On account of successive bad seasons many had lately been turned out of their holdings. There were agrarian riots and a reign of terror in many parts of Ireland. Of late a party had arisen in Parliament known as the Irish Home Rulers who hoped to get Home Rule for Ireland by obstructing all business in Parliament not connected with Ireland. Gladstone met the situation by passing a second Land Act which established a court to fix rents which were in dispute. He also passed measures to put down murder and outrage, as a result of which, the Home Rulers joined the Conservatives in 1885 and drove Gladstone out of power. The Conservatives then took office under Lord Salisbury.

The new ministry did not last long, for next year the Home Rulers discovering that Gladstone was favourable to Home Rule, threw their entire weight into the scale with his party and Lord Salisbury's government fell.

Irish Home Rule Bill.

Gladstone now felt that Home Rule was the only means of satisfying the Irish and at once introduced his First Home Rule Bill by which Ireland was to have a

Parliament of her own. The Bill met with great opposition, even amongst his own followers, and was rejected. Many of the Liberals deserted Gladstone, to be henceforth known as the Liberal Unionists, the chief among them being Joseph Chamberlain. They joined the ranks of the Conservatives to form what is called the Unionist Party. At the next election in 1886 the Home Rulers or Gladstonians were beaten and the Unionists formed a ministry under Lord Salisbury.

Unionist Ministry, 1886—1892.

Several measures were passed both to satisfy the Irish people and repress Irish discontent and for a time Ireland was at peace.

In 1887 the Queen completed the 50th year of her reign and, to commemorate the event, the First Jubilee was celebrated with unparalleled enthusiasm throughout the British Empire. Ten years later took place the Diamond Jubilee of the Queen who had then reigned for sixty years. The rejoicings on these occasions did much to strengthen the feelings of unity between England and her possessions abroad.

Gladstone's last Ministry, Second Home Rule Bill.

In 1892 Gladstone returned to power, when the Unionist Ministry, rendered unpopular by its strong measures in Ireland, was defeated by the Home Rulers throwing their entire weight on the Liberal side. Gladstone introduced a new Home Rule Bill which passed in the House of Commons but was thrown out in the House of Lords. Gladstone now retired from public life and died four years later, at the age of eighty-eight, in the midst of national sorrow. For more than a quarter of a century, he had along with his great opponent Disraeli dominated British politics. The greatest orator and financier of his age, he was at the same time a great 'moral force.' A high purpose—to serve the public good—shone through all his actions and to him politics was no hobby but a serious duty. When he died it appeared to many that 'the light seemed to have died out of the sky.'

The Unionist Ministry of 1896.

The election of 1895 gave the Unionists a majority and they remained in power till the Queen's death. The first important task undertaken was the re-conquest of the Sudan which was completed in 1898.

The Boer War.

Affairs in South Africa, however, proved more difficult to tackle. Since the Transvaal had been granted its independence in 1881 conditions had changed. The discovery of gold-fields in 1885 had attracted large numbers of immigrants mostly British. They were badly treated by the Boers who taxed them heavily, but gave them no rights of citizenship. They therefore formed a plot against the Boers, which fared miserably, but which made a peaceful solution of the Transvaal problem impossible. War broke out in October 1899. The Boers besieged Kimberley and Mafeking and the British troops at Natal under Sir George White, after a fortnight's hard fighting, were driven into Ladysmith where they held out for 118 days. Mafeking was being ably defended by Col. Baden-Powell (now Sir Robert Baden-Powell, founder of the Boy Scout movement). This siege lasted for 218 days and the day of its relief was one of great joy throughout the Empire.

Early attempts of the additional troops sent to relieve the besieged towns were unsuccessful. In the space of one week (between December 10 and 17, 1899) the British suffered three defeats, and it seemed as if the Boers were going to win the day. The whole of Britain was aroused. On all sides men offered their services and large reinforcements were despatched. Early in 1900 Lord Roberts and Lord Kitchener were sent to the scene of war. Now the whole situation changed. By February 15, Kimberley was relieved, and on February 27 the main Boer army under Cronje surrendered to Lord Roberts. By March 3, General Buller had relieved Ladysmith and on May 17 a squadron of British troops reached Mafeking and compelled the Boers to raise the siege of that place. By October, the Transvaal and the Orange Free State, the neighbouring Boer republic, had been annexed to the British Empire, the latter under the name of the Orange River Colony. Roving bands of the Boers carried on guerilla warfare for more than a year. But Lord Kitchener, who was left to finish the war and make the country quiet and peaceful again, proved more than a match for their tactics. He planned an elaborate system of block houses to make the railway lines safe. Little by little the number of the enemy grew less by

LORD KITCHENER

capture, wounds or death. At last, peace was made in 1902 by which the Boers agreed to submit and become subjects of the British sovereign. All the States of South Africa, British and Dutch, have since been combined into one great Dominion, the Union of South Africa, having one Parliament in which Britons and Boers sit together (1910).

Colonial Expansion.

We have seen how Cape Colony came to the British early in the 19th century and how the Transvaal and the Orange River Colony were annexed after the Boer War. But this does not finish the story of colonial expansion during Victoria's reign. Canada, conquered by Wolfe in 1759, had been a French colony. Gradually there was British immigration and by the time the Queen ascended the throne the country had two distinct divisions—Upper Canada inhabited almost entirely by people of British origin and Lower Canada the population of which was almost entirely of French descent. Strife went on between the British and the French Colonists till 1867 when the federation of the two parts into one Dominion of Canada took place and they learnt to live peaceably together. New provinces as they grew stronger were added and before the Queen died 'the little British possession of 1759, described by the French as a few square miles of snow had grown till she was thirty times the size of the mother-country.' The first footing of the British in the island-continent of Australia was made when Captain Cook discovered it and placed on its soil the flag of his royal master.

King George III. At first a settlement for convicts, it grew in importance through the discovery of goldfields in 1851, which attracted large numbers of immigrants. Many colonies were set up in different parts of the country which were united in 1901 to form the Australian Commonwealth.

The Death of the Queen.

The great Queen passed away on January 22, 1901, full of years and glory. Hers had been a long reign—longer than that of any other English sovereign. But it is not by its length alone that the Victorian period stands unique in English history. It was a period of wonderful progress in all directions. The population of the British Isles trebled and the area under England's sway grew four times as large as it was at the Queen's accession. The lot of the wage-earners improved considerably. They had less work and more wages now, and were better housed and better fed. There were rapid advances in transport. At the time when Victoria came to the throne, twenty miles an hour was considered to be a reckless speed for a railway train; sixty years later, expresses were running at more than sixty miles an hour with perfect safety. The steamship and the electric telegraph served to annihilate distance and British trade grew immensely during these years. Progress in the realms of science was not less marvellous. The telescope, the telephone, the electric light were all the achievements of this period. In 1859, after a close study of plant and animal life, Darwin gave to the world 'The Origin of Species'—a book which revolutionised all old ideas on Nature and Man. The introduction of ether and chloroform and the discovery of X-rays widened the possibilities of surgery. The Victorian era made no mean contribution to literature as well. Dickens and Thackeray, Tennyson and Browning, Carlyle and Macaulay are great names. The latter is well-known in Indian history for his famous 'Education Minute,' and as the author of the Indian Penal Code.

CHAPTER XVII

EDWARD VII

1901—1910

When King Edward came to the throne in 1901 at the age of 59, he noticed, shrewd and wise as he was, that the leading nations of Europe were living in a state of tension, suspecting one another's designs. The South African War had also created much sore feeling and misunderstanding of England on the Continent. The most important work which awaited him therefore was to bring about friendly feelings with and among European Powers and in this he succeeded admirably during his short reign of nine years.

He had travelled extensively in Europe, America, and distant parts of the British Empire. This had taught him to look at things from a broader point of view. Again, he was a kinsman of most of the ruling monarchs of Europe. His Queen, Alexandra, was a princess of Denmark, the Queen of Norway was his daughter, the Emperor of Germany was his nephew, the Tzarina of Russia, the Queen of Spain, the Crown Princess of Sweden were his nieces. The French therefore sometimes called him 'the uncle of Europ

The Coronation ceremony, originally fixed for June 24, 1902 was postponed, owing to the King's illness which necessitated an operation, and was performed on August 9, 1902.

Soon after, King Edward began to use his great ability and influence for preserving peace in Europe and securing the friendship of foreign powers with England. His great tact and genial manners, uniform courtesy and unfailing hospitality made him a popular sovereign.

Relations with Foreign Powers.

He conceived the happy idea of making official visits to the Continental powers. In 1903, he paid a State visit to Paris. This was quickly followed by a visit of the French President to England. The interchange of visits had a healthy and beneficial effect.

Friendship between England and France grew apace, and in 1904 was signed the *Anglo-French Agreement*, known as the *Entente Cordiale* which settled all differences between England and France about Egypt and Morocco. A friendly alliance was made with Japan in 1902 and in 1905 was signed the *Anglo-Japanese Treaty* by which either power agreed to help the other in case of an unprovoked war. This treaty, as we shall see later on, made Japan take the side of England in the Great World War. The Anglo-Russian Convention (1907) settled the old dispute between England and Russia in Persia and Afghanistan. This was followed in 1908 and 1909 by meetings between the King and the Tzar to cement friendship. Apart from treaties and alliances, important powers met together several times to discuss matters relating to international peace and this prevented many a war. In every case the influence of King Edward was visibly felt and he rightly earned the title of "Edward the Peacemaker." Germany alone remained aloof and did not agree to his proposals of mutual friendship. So great was the popularity of King Edward abroad that his funeral procession (1910) was personally attended by no less than nine ruling sovereigns.

If King Edward did so well in securing for England the friendship and regard of the great powers of the world, he was no less successful at home. Coming to the throne after Queen Victoria, whom the people had almost adored, it was no small thing for the King to succeed in gaining their esteem and affection. At the time of his accession he had declared 'I am fully determined to be a Constitutional sovereign in the strictest sense of the word and as long as there is breath in my body, to work for the amelioration and good of my people.' And that promise he nobly fulfilled. He never showed any party preferences for he recognised that he represented the nation and it was not for him to take sides. The result was that during his reign, the system of party-government was highly developed. He showed great interest in the affairs of the country and the people felt proud of him.

There was no change in Ministry when Queen Victoria died and King Edward VII succeeded to the throne (1901). Lord Salisbury, now an old man of over seventy, continued to be Premier. But soon after the conclusion of the treaty with the Boers (May 1902), he decided to retire. He resigned (July 1902) and his place was taken by his nephew A. J. Balfour. Of late the Conservative party had ceased to be popular. The South African War had involved a great drain of men and money on England, for which the Government of Lord Salisbury was held largely responsible. The Government also acted unwisely in permitting cheap Chinese labour to be imported into South Africa to get the gold mines in working order. The conditions of service under which these labourers were brought made the English people suspect that the Government was countenancing a form of slavery. But the real thing which caused a split in Mr. Balfour's party was the Tariff Reform advocated by Mr. Chamberlain, the then Secretary of State for Colonies.

Tariff Reform.

In 1903, Mr. Chamberlain paid a visit to South Africa to discuss personally with the government the question regarding the future development of that Colony. On his return home he suggested that Colonies should have preference in their trade with the mother country. This, he explained, could be done by imposing higher taxes on all foreign goods that entered English ports than in the case of goods sent by the British Colonies. The policy of 'Imperial Preference,' as it is called, revived the old controversy of Free-Trade *versus* Protection, which had engaged the attention of statesmen and thinkers in the time of Sir Robert Peel. We have seen that towards the middle of the nineteenth century the Corn Laws had to be repealed and protective duties abolished in order to make bread cheap enough for poor people. Since 1846 England had been progressively a Free Trade country and during these years her trade had enormously increased and she had become one of the wealthiest nations of the world. The people were not prepared to believe that Free Trade, which had made England so prosperous, was a wrong policy. They could not forget that protection which had once been tried had brought much misery to the poor people. They did not like the idea of any tax being levied upon food and a tax on foreign corn was a necessary part of Mr. Chamberlain's scheme. The Liberals were in favour of Free-Trade, while the Unionists, as led by Mr. Chamberlain, stood for Tariff Reform.

In 1906, when the General Election took place, the Unionists, who had already lost much of their popularity on account of the South African War and the importation of Chinese labour, suffered a severe defeat. The Liberals, who had Sir Henry Campbell Bannerman as their leader, were returned to power with a large majority.

Some measures passed by the Liberal Government.

The new Government at once set to work on a large programme of social reform, which aimed at the economic well-being of the people. An Act was passed which permitted municipal and county councils to collect and spend money for the proper feeding of school children (1906). The Old Age Pensions Act (1908) allowed every one who was seventy years of age or more to claim from the Government 5 s. a week, provided he had less than £28 a year. In 1910, the National Health Insurance system was established. Every worker earning less than £100 a year was compelled to pay as his contribution four pence a week out of his wages, the employer paid another five pence and the state threepence. Out of this fund payments are made to workers who fall ill. The Bill for the Protection of Children and Miners Eight Hours Bill were also passed in 1908—Acts which greatly improved the position of the labouring classes and strengthened the position of Trade Unions. The Army and Navy were reorganised to make them more efficient for purposes of national defence.

Budget of 1909.

All these schemes involved a huge expenditure. The Government had tried to keep expenditure within the income and to avoid deficit-budgets. But the Budget of 1909 showed an enormous increase in expenditure. To meet this the Government proposed an increase in the income tax and land tax. The Budget passed the Commons, but the Lords with great vested interests in land, regarded the increase in the land-tax as unfair and rejected the Budget. The Lords as well as the Unionists argued that the changes proposed by the Government were of too radical a nature to be accepted before the electors had an opportunity of expressing their opinion on them.

For many years the Lords had not interfered with budgets on the ground that it was not their concern, because most of the revenue was paid by the common people. The Government, therefore, considered this rejection of the Budget by the Lords quite unjustifiable. The Liberals appealed to the country. The elections held in January 1910 went again in favour of the Liberals. The Lords then passed the Budget of 1909.

The Government now brought forward the Parliament Bill. It aimed at restricting and curtailing the powers of the House of Lords in rejecting Bills passed by the House of Commons. While the Bill was being debated in the House of Commons, the King was suddenly taken ill. In a few days he died (May 6, 1910).

The Parliament Act, 1911.

The Premier, Mr. Asquith, who had succeeded Sir H. Campbell Bannerman after his death in 1908, could not quite decently ask the new King (George V) to use his Royal Prerogative in the first few months of his reign to create new Peers to overcome any opposition. It was agreed therefore that a Conference of party leaders should be held to see if some compromise could be effected. The failure of the Conference led to a decision to appeal once again to the country. The election of December 1910 gave the Government the same majority as before. This time, when the Bill was sent to the House of Lords, most of the Peers abstained from voting and the Parliament Act was passed in August 1911 without any difficulty. It provides that any Bill which has passed in three successive sessions of the House of Commons shall become Law, notwithstanding the opposition of the House of Lords. The House of Lords is deprived of the power of rejecting or amending any money bill, *i.e.*, a proposal for raising money to meet the Government expenditure. This was a great triumph for the Commons. The Parliament Act of 1911 is an important landmark in the history of England.

Ireland, 1893—1914.

After the failure of Home Rule Bill in 1893, the question of Ireland did not seriously trouble the Government. The enthusiasm of all parties seemed to have considerably cooled down. The Unionists believed that by giving good administration, which should better the condition of peasants, the Irish would in due course of time be reconciled to the Act of Union. Their policy had a considerable measure of success.

Co-operative Societies and Banks.

In 1894 the Irish Agricultural Organisation Society was started. It had nothing to do with politics. Its main object was to teach the Irish peasants and farmers to help themselves. Local Co-operative societies were started in many places. The Irish farmers soon learnt that it was far more economical to buy seeds and implements by joining together than by doing so individually. The Co-operative societies could also sell their produce at more profit. The new Co-operative banks could lend them money at favourable rates of interests and save them from the oppression of usurers. And this had a very healthy effect on small farmers. They were now much better off and the wave of emigration from Ireland was checked.

The Wyndham Act of 1903.

The Wyndham Act proved a veritable blessing to the farmer. It aimed at enabling tenants to acquire private property. Under its provisions, the British Government was to advance a huge sum (£100,000,000) to Ireland. This money was to be used in purchasing Irish estates. The landlords were not compelled to sell, but they were offered a good price for their estates. The estates thus purchased were divided into small fields and sold to peasants, who could pay the price to Government by small annual payments spread over 68½ years. There was nothing easier for the farmer than to pay the Government year by year with the money they made by the land. This process enabled the Irish peasantry to acquire many thousands of acres of land. The peasant proprietors became fairly prosperous and firmly settled on their land.

The Third Home Rule Bill, 1914.

The Liberal Government was sympathetic towards the demand of the Nationalists for Home Rule. The fact that the Liberals in spite of their open advocacy of Home Rule were returned to power in the last two General Elections, showed that the majority of the English people did not disapprove of it. Three times successively the Bill passed the House of Commons and every time did the House of Lords reject it. At last under the provisions of the Parliament Act of 1911, it passed in 1914 by the consent of the King and Commons.

The Ulstermen or people in the north of Ireland, most of whom are Protestants, announced that they would never submit to the Home Rule. They began to arm themselves. The Irish Nationalists, who had struggled so long and so hard to get Home Rule, were equally prepared to oppose them. Mr. Bonar Law, the leader of the Unionist party, had publicly promised to support the Ulstermen. The Government was taking no steps to suppress either party. A conference of political leaders at Buckingham Palace failed to arrive at any agreement and civil war in Ireland seemed to be imminent. The outbreak of the Great World War reunited the nation. By a compromise, the Home Rule Act was not to be brought into force till it was over.

A few more matters deserve a passing mention in connection with the reign of King Edward VII. The Boy Scout movement was started by General Sir Robert Baden-Powell. The educated women of England started what is known as the Suffragette movement demanding the right of voting for women. Lord Haldane's Bill in 1907 created the Territorial Force, formed a Special Militia Reserve, and provided for an Officers' Training Corps. Only one far-sighted soldier, Lord Roberts, saw the weakness of the Home Defences. The Indian Councils Act (1903) was passed by the British

Parliament, which gave to the Indians more scope in the Civil Service and greater share in the various provincial Legislative Councils. The Russo-Japanese War (1904-1905), though it did not directly concern the English people, aroused especial interest, since Japan had become an ally of England. Japan was for the first time recognised as a country of first-rate military importance and became a great world power.

During the period 1901—1910 the country was, on the whole, prosperous. People could get plentiful work and necessaries of life were comparatively cheap. Wages were steadily rising. The use of motor cars and electricity as a driving power was becoming common. But the expenditure on armaments increased at a rapid rate.

Conclusion.

There are two events of outstanding importance in the reign of King Edward, which give him a prominent place among English sovereigns.

(*a*) *The Union of South Africa,* which resulted from the generous policy of the Liberal Government. A long and bitter war had been concluded in 1902, yet, in 1910, the four States (Cape Colony, Natal, Transvaal, and Orange Free State) of their own free will agreed to bury the past and the Boers and the Britons resolved to work together for the good of the whole country.

(*b*) *Diplomatic relations* with foreign powers, towards the success of which the personality of the King was a notable factor. The next chapter will explain how the course of the Great World War was effected and modified by these international treaties and alliances.

CHAPTER XVIII

GEORGE V

After the death of King Edward VII, his second son came to the throne as King George V (1910). Some of the events relating to this period have already been mentioned. The Parliament Act was passed in 1911 and the Home Rule Act in 1914. George V was the first English King to come out to India to be crowned at Delhi (1912) as our King-Emperor. But by far the most important event is the Great World War which broke out on August 4, 1914. In order to understand why England was drawn into this War, so soon after the death of King Edward VII who had striven so hard to preserve the peace of Europe, it is necessary to know what was going on in Germany, Austria-Hungary and the Balkan States.

England and Germany.

From 1870 to 1910 most of the countries of Europe had enjoyed a long spell of peace. During this period great progress was made in applying scientific methods to the production of manufactured goods. Thus labour-saving inventions and improved transport produced an ever-increasing volume of commerce and international trade. Nations vied with each other in selling their goods all over the world, in competing for old markets and creating fresh ones. This created ill-will between the countries which were most active and ambitious. Germany and England, the foremost nations of Europe, were for this reason becoming more and more jealous of each other. The lack of friendly feelings became quite apparent when the Kaiser (the Emperor of Germany), sent a telegram to the President of the Boers, congratulating him on his success in the early stages of the Boer War. But a clearer proof of Germany's designs lay in her building a huge navy, though she had not a very large coast to defend. In 1912, a proposal was made to Germany that she should not go on adding to her fleet, as such a step would obviously be aimed at England. This the German Government refused to agree to, unless England bound herself to be neutral in the event of a European War. Now that was an impossible condition, bound as England was by treaty obligations to France and Russia.

Germany and France.

As Germany had come into power and prominence rather late, she found that other European Powers had captured the markets in the most desirable parts of the outer world. The few colonies which she had acquired were unprofitable and offered no attraction to the Germans to settle there. The Kaiser made an attempt in 1905, and again in 1911 to further the interests of Germany in Morocco and drive out France from there, but each time his plan failed on account of the intervention of England.

Middle Europe. Having failed to find a footing on the north coast of Africa, Germany began to think of other territory nearer home. She dreamed of a 'Middle Europe' to be controlled by herself. By the Triple Alliance of 1882 Germany, Austria-Hungary and Italy had bound themselves to help one another, if any of them should be attacked by Russia or by any other Power which had the help of Russia. If the Balkan States and Turkey should come under the influence of Germany, she would get a safe passage to the Nearer and Farther East. The Kaiser had a marvellous success in Turkey. The Sultan, as a result of the Balkan Wars, had lost his European territory very considerably. The Kaiser paid visits to Constantinople and Jerusalem and posed as Protector of the Muslim World. German capital found its way unchecked into Turkey and German officers trained the Turkish armies. German engineers had built a railway from Berlin which was designed to link up Baghdad and the Indian Ocean. Only the last stages remained to be completed and German influence in Turkey was so great that this could be done at any time. Only the weak Balkan States, which had lately become independent of Turkey, remained to be won over. Of these Bulgaria, Rumania and Macedonia were quite friendly. Only Serbia remained. If she did not prove amenable to German or Austro-Hugarian influence and showed a leaning towards Russia, she was to be crushed at the first opportunity.

This accomplished, a huge German Empire in the East seemed to be a possibility.

Herzegovina and Bosnia.

Now, Serbia is a country of Slavs. Close to Serbia on the Adriatic Coast there are two small provinces, Herzegovina and Bosnia, which have a large element of Slav population; but since 1878, the Austrians had taken over their control and had finally annexed them (1908). The Serbians greatly resented this. The Slavs naturally looked to Russia as their leader as she, too, has a large Slav population. They appealed to Russia to help them, but on account of her defeat in the Russo-Japanese War (1904-1905) she did not find herself strong enough to intervene, because that might have brought on war with Austria who had the strong support of Germany.

Failing to get help from Russia, the Serbians formed a secret society which aimed at the separation of Bosnia and Herzegovina from Austria-Hungary and their inclusion in Serbia. Their propaganda had caused a bitter hatred of Austrians among the Slav population. On June 28, 1914, the Archduke Ferdinand, heir to the Austrian throne, and his wife were murdered at Sarajevo, the capital of Bosnia. The Austrian Government conducted an investigation and alleged that the murderers, who were Bosnians, belonged to the Serbian secret society and had been aided by Serbian officials.

On July 23, Austria-Hungary sent a note to the Serbian Government demanding a fulfilment of conditions, which would have practically cost them their independence. Forty-eight hours were allowed for the unconditional acceptance or rejection of the terms. The Serbian Government was prepared to accept most of the conditions but not all. They proposed that the whole question should be referred to the International Conference at The Hague for arbitration, but Austria-Hungary rejected the Serb reply as unsatisfactory and on July 28, 1914 declared war upon her little neighbour.

War declared on Serbia.

Russia, the protector of the Slavs of the Balkans, could not sit idly, while Austria tried to destroy the independence of Serbia. But if Russia came in to help Serbia by making war on Austria-Hungary, then Germany, bound by the Triple Alliance, would surely attack Russia: and France, bound to Russia in the same way, would be obliged to attack Germany. A general European war seemed to be threatening. Great Britain, through Sir Edward Grey, Secretary for Foreign Affairs, tried her best to bring about some peaceful settlement, but Germany declared that the whole dispute concerned only Austria-Hungary and Serbia and that Russia should not be a party to it. If Russia interfered, Germany would back her ally, Austria-Hungary. As soon as the news came that the Austrians were attacking Serbia, Russia began to mobilize her armies on the entire Western border

Germany declares war on Russia and France.

of her great Empire. Russian mobilization gave Germany a pretext for interference. The Kaiser's Government, accordingly, sent an ultimatum to Russia requiring that country to withdraw her troops within twelve hours or accept the consequences. Russia did not reply and the Kaiser declared war on Russia (August 1). France, too, began to mobilize and Germany declared war on France (August 3).

War declared by England.

On August 2, Germany addressed a note to Belgium asking permission to move troops across the country into France and threatening, in case of refusal, to leave Belgium's fate to the "decision of arms." The Belgian Government, under King Albert, declined to "sacrifice the honour of the nation and betray its duty towards Europe." On August 4, German troops crossed the frontier of Belgium to attack France. This was in violation of a solemn treaty, to which Germany and other European powers had pledged themselves, and which Germany now regarded 'a scrap of paper.' Moreover this move of Germany threatened to give her navy the possession of the channel ports opposite Dover and the Thames. Immediately Great Britain called upon Germany to withdraw and "play fair." Refusal left Britain no choice but to declare war on the breaker of treaties since she, too, had guaranteed the neutrality of Belgium.

Turkey also joins Germany.

Turkey, largely controlled by Germany and fearful of Russia's advance on Constantinople, soon joined the

Central Powers (Germany and Austria-Hungary). Her entry into the war did not at first greatly affect the situation, for she was cut off from her allies by Bulgaria, which was still neutral and Serbia, which was hostile. The Sultan declared a holy war against the 'enemies of Islam.' Contrary to German hopes, the Muslims of North Africa, Egypt and India instead of revolting fought loyally for England and France.

The Balkan States. Some of the Balkan States sided with the Central Powers, others fought against them, but by the end of August 1916, the hostile states were all conquered by the Austrian and German troops, and their communication with Turkey was free.

Italy. Italy declared neutrality in 1914 on the ground that the terms of the Triple Alliance did not bind her to assist the Central Powers in an offensive war, but she could not remain neutral. The pressure of national interests urged Italy to side with the Allies and against Central Powers.

Course of the War. Germany's plan of campaign was to march troops quickly across Belgium into France, occupy Paris and the Channel ports and then use her great army in conjunction with Austria and Turkey to crush the slow-moving and hesitating Russians and last of all to deal with Great Britain. She might have succeeded but for the unexpected opposition offered by Belgium and the quick decision of Russia to mobilize her forces. The stubborn and heroic fight put up by the Belgians delayed the progress of German troops into France. The success of Russia on the eastern border of Prussia and Austria-Hungary made it necessary for Germany to withdraw some of her troops from the Western Front (Belgium and France) and send them to the Eastern Front to check the Russian advance. The withdrawal of troops from the Western Front and resistance offered by the Belgians enabled the Allies (England and France), who were unprepared for war, to bring their forces into the field before the enemy had advanced far into France. England declared war on August 4, and by the end of that month she landed her troops in France under Sir John French. They were just in time to take their place in the French line near Mons. The French and English troops retreated before the onrush of the enemy but saved Paris. For about 4 years after this, huge armies, occupying a line about six hundred miles long on the Western Front, fought now and then pitched battles of great severity resulting in the loss of hundreds of thousands of lives on either side, but more often fought in trenches, continuously bombarding and surprising the enemy by night-attacks and the use of poison-gas. The most important battles fought on the Western Front by the end of 1917 were on the Marne, Verdun, the Somme and Ypres.

On the Eastern Front the Russians, who had considerably advanced into the enemy's country, retreated very quickly before the German troops led by Marshal Von Hindenburg—now (1927)

President of the German Republic. In 1917, there was a Revolution in Russia. She could no longer fight the enemy and in March 1918, she signed a surrender-peace treaty with Germany. The defeat of Russia now left most of the German troops free to take their place on the Western Front.

Fighting was not confined merely to the Western and Eastern Fronts. In Mesopotamia the Turks had inflicted a severe blow by the capture of Kut (April 1916) but the British forces under Sir Stanley Maude recovered the lost ground, and took Baghdad in 1917. The Turks attempted to cross the Suez Canal and reach Egypt, but the attack failed and at the end of 1917 General Allenby captured Jerusalem. Fighting was also going on in the mountainous north-east of Italy to the advanatge of the Allies. British, Indian and South African forces robbed Germany of her Colonies in Africa. Japan had occupied Kiauchau, Germany's Colony in China, soon after the outbreak of the war.

The Navy.

There were few serious naval actions. England's food supply and the transport of her armies to France and distant fields were secured by the ceaseless watch and work of her Navy. The enemy warships were safe behind their mine fields in the Kiel Canal. The German fleet ventured out only occasionally and succeeded in bombarding Hartlepool and Scarborough in November 1914. The Emden bombarded Madras but was soon captured by an Australian cruiser. In May 1916, the battle of Jutland was fought. The victory was indecisive and the losses on either side were very heavy.

In the beginning of 1915, the British troops had tried to force their way up the Dardanelles in order to help Russia from the South, but the Peninsula was strongly held by Turkish troops under the direction of German officers. The British losses were heavy and progress was slow. In December 1915, the British Government decided to abandon the scheme and the troops were safely withdrawn.

The German weapon of attack at sea was the submarine, which sank many merchant vessels, transport and passenger ships. On January 31, the German Government declared an unrestricted blockade of Great Britain, that is, any ship, Allied or neutral, sailing to British ports was to be sunk at sight. This policy seriously affected the position of Great Britain. The loss of merchant vessels grew heavier and heavier every month. In order to cause panic among the civil population, the Germans sent aeroplane raiders to bomb London and other towns, almost nightly. The most difficult problem was the supply of food. This was solved by the Government by putting a rationing system into force, which secured plain but sufficient food to every individual.

The United States of America enter the War.

The unrestricted submarine warfare elicited a protest from the United States of America, because it was a clear violation of the rights of America to the freedom of the high seas.

Germany did not pay any heed to this protest. This action of Germany forced the United States of America to side with the Allies. In 1917 the situation seemed to be far from hopeful. Russia had dropped out from the struggle. German troops still occupied a considerable part of Belgium and France. France was overstrained, mutinous outbreaks were frequent in her army, and her material resources were almost exhausted. Austro-German troops had driven Italy back almost to the gates of Venice. German submarines still took terrific toll of English merchantmen. Many people had begun to feel that it was impossible to win and struggle was not worth the sacrifice. But the entry of the United States of America into the War greatly changed the outlook. She had previously been of great assistance to the Allies in furnishing vast quantities of munitions, food and stores of all kinds. She came in finally to uphold "the principles of peace and justice" and "to make the whole world safe for democracy."

Last effort of Germany.

Germany, therefore, resolved to make her last big effort on the Western Front. Half a million men and thousands of big guns were brought from Russia and Italy. On March 21, the storm burst, and the Allies were compelled to fall back before the German onrush. The British line was broken at St. Quentin and much of the ground gained and held as the result of so many battles during the last four years was lost. There was a general retreat but no rout, the armies fought steadily as they went back. The

MARSHAL FOCH

Allied line was forced back to the Marne. It seemed as if the work of the British armies done during the last four years had been undone by the enemy in one month.

It was then that the wisest possible move was made by putting all the Allied troops under one Commander, the French Marshal Foch. By counter-attacks, Marshal Foch had tried to find out weak points in the enemy's lines. At last, by the free use of a large and daily increasing American army, he succeeded in stopping the German advance at Amiens (April 26, 1918). He was now convinced that the Germans had strained themselves just too far and beyond their strength.

July 18 was the turning point in the struggle. It was on that memorable day that Marshal Foch began the counter-offensive, which proved to be his master-stroke. The enemy had never expected that the Allies after their long and continuous retreat would undertake an offensive. Blows were struck so rapidly and with such force at different points of the line that the Germans had no sooner rushed up reinforcements at one spot than they were needed at another. Now it was the turn of the Germans to retreat. They too fought steadily to the end and retreated without panic. This great Allied pressure continued unrelaxed till the final victory. The revolution in the German fleet in the Kiel Canal was a clear proof that Germany was no longer able to bear the strain of the war. On April 23, Zeebrugge, the chief base of the German submarines, had been blown up.

If all this was bad for Germany, her associates were worse off. The Bulgarians were forced to make peace on September 30, and the Turks finding themselves helpless against the rapid advance of General Allenby signed an armistice on October 30.

On October 24, the British troops helped by the Italian and French forces opened a great offensive against the Austrians on the Italian Front. The Austrian armies melted into hopeless rout. On November 4, Austria signed an armistice. A revolution was already breaking out in her capital Vienna.

The End. The Kaiser finding his allies give way one after the other felt that the game was up. On November 9, he abdicated and, with the Crown Prince, fled to Holland where he still lives. By November 10, the English army ably led by Haig had driven the Germans back at Mons over the line from which they themselves had retreated in 1914. On November 11, the Armistice was signed with Germany and the War came to an end. On November 21, the German fleet steamed out from its hiding place to surrender to the Allies.

Cost of the War. The British Empire alone lost about a million men and over 9,000 million pounds sterling was spent in the conduct of the War.

Some important features of the War. Never before in the recorded history of the world had so many nations taken an active part in a war and never before had a war been fought on such a gigantic scale. It is estimated that about six crores of men were mobilized and the number of casualties was 3⅓ crores of which more than ¾ crores were certainly killed. The direct cost of the war to the fighting nations was over Rs. 5,20,80,00,00,000. Aeroplanes and Wireless were for the first time used in this war and played a very important part. The war gave a great impetus to the development of the destructive weapons of war. Long-range guns, tanks, poison-gas, and submarines are only a few of the deadlier things that were used in this War.

The British Empire.

The war was forced on the English at a time when the storm of a civil war was threatening in Ireland. The enemy hoped that Great Britain would find it difficult to carry on war and at the same time to keep together her vast Dominions. But the ready response and unstinted help offered by her Colonies and Dominions throughout this crisis proved beyond any shadow of doubt that the British Empire was sound at heart. While every individual, who did his little bit for King and country, is responsible for bringing about the final victory, two personalities emerge from the host, Lord Kitchener and Mr. Lloyd George. Lord Kitchener had seen at an early stage that the struggle would be prolonged. To him must go the credit of raising and training the New Armies of England. He was drowned off the Orkneys, when on his way to Russia. Lloyd George was the heart and soul of the Government throughout the period of war. As

DAVID LLOYD GEORGE

Minister of Munitions, he had done splendid and wonderful work. As Prime Minister, he inspired the English nation with his fervent zeal. He never doubted that Great Britain would win and the nation had faith in him that he could win. It was he who kept up the spirit of the people in the darkest days of the struggle. And when the war was over, he would accept no honour or reward He simply holds the Order of Merit (O. M.), the order established by King Edward VII to celebrate his Coronation (1902).

The Treaty of Versailles.

On January 18, 1919, the Peace Conference assembled at Paris, to settle the terms of peace with the Central Powers. After prolonged discussion, a treaty was drawn up and delivered to German delegates. They tried to secure important changes in its terms, but the Allies told them firmly that Germany should either accept the terms unconditionally or the war would be renewed. On June 28, the treaty was signed at Versailles.

The important terms of the treaty were: (1) Alsace and Lorraine were returned to France: (2) the German Empire lost all her Colonies; (3) Poland and Czecho-Slavakia were recognised as new and independent States: (4) Germany was to pay reparation for the damage caused by the war; Similar treaties were offered to Austria, Hungary, Bulgaria and Turkey and signed by them. The territories of these countries were greatly reduced and many small nationalities, which were held in subjection by the Central Powers, were established as Independent States.

The League of Nations.

But perhaps the most important work achieved by the Conference was the founding of the League of Nations, which was largely due to Mr. Woodrow Wilson, President of the United States of America. The League of Nations or the Parliament of Nations has for its object the settling of disputes between nations before they resort to fighting. Its members cannot make secret treaties and alliances. It has a permanent Secretariat at Geneva, Switzerland. Every year a meeting is held at Geneva for the discussion of International questions. All important decisions require a unanimous vote, though it is not binding on the members to accept the decisions of the League. It is expected that the League will greatly reduce the chances of another Great World War, because a member of the League declaring war against the wishes of the League, must take into consideration the fact that other members of the League would be ranged against him. At present almost all the great nations of the world excepting America are members of the League.

Gains to the British Empire.

While the Great World War established the position of England as the wealthiest and most powerful nation of Europe, it also greatly strengthened her position as an Imperial Power. She obtained Cyprus and the bulk of German Colonies and assumed the government of Palestine and Iraq. She confirmed her sovereignty over the Anglo-Egyptian Sudan and established a protectorate over the new Arab

State of Hedjaz. In her own Dominions, the war has greatly enhanced her prestige.

1914—1927.

Coalition Government.

For carrying on the war successfully it was considered necessary that the Government should not only be representative of the majority of people but also popular. In 1915 a Coalition Government was formed, under Mr. Asquith, including the Unionist and Labour leaders. Mr. Lloyd George was the Munitions Minister. The Asquith Government passed the Conscription Acts, which required every able-bodied man between 18 and 45 years to enlist himself in the army, navy, or air force. This kept up the strength of the New Armies. In 1916, Mr. Lloyd George became the Premier. The new Government took all mines, railways, farms and ships, under its control. As raids of zeppelin airships were becoming frequent over London and other towns, strict orders were issued that all lights should be put out soon after it was evening.

Sinn Fein.

In Ireland an extreme party had appeared, known as Sinn Fein ("Ourselves alone"), and in Easter, 1916, there was a rebellion in Dublin. The rebellion was the more serious as it occurred during the war, but it was easily suppressed. The leader, Roger Casement, who was financed by the German authorities, was captured on landing in Ireland from a small boat and was afterwards executed.

HERBERT HENRY ASQUITH

In 1918, soon after the war was over, a Representation of the People Act was passed, which gave practically every young man at the age of 21 and every woman above 30 the right to vote at the polls. This was done in recognition of the services of the men who had fought and the women who had served in hospitals, factories, and in many other capacities.

Representation of the People Act.

A similar recognition of war services was made in the case of India, when the Government of India Act (1919) was passed. It increased the non-official majority in the Legislative Assembly and transferred some responsibility to Ministers in the Provinces. It was a first step towards the grant of responsible Government to India.

Government of India Act.

The new election held under the Representation of the People Act (1918) again returned Lloyd George to power by a very large majority. But he had soon to face a situation, which proved more difficult than war problems. There was lack of money in the country, while taxation had already reached a limit beyond which it could not go. Necessaries of life were getting dearer and employers were unwilling to raise wages, because of trade depression. The Government could not give effect to any reforms for lack of funds; industrial disputes, ending in the Coal and Railway strikes of 1919-1920, became very serious affairs, and unemployment increased beyond all estimates. The people thought a coalition of opposite parties could sot solve their difficulties. The Government resigned, and, in the new election, the Conservatives were returned to power (1922).

Return to Party Government.

The new Premier, Mr. Bonar Law, had to retire after a few months because of ill-health (he died in 1923). His place was taken by Mr. Baldwin. The new Premier thought that the right solution of all difficulties lay in reviving Protection. He sought a new election (1923) to find if the country was in favour of introducing that measure. The result was that the Liberal Party which had always advocated Free Trade and the Labour Party were returned in a majority. In January 1924 Mr. Ramsay Macdonald, the Labour leader, became the first Labour Premier.

The Labour Government had no more success than the Conservative one in dealing with unemployment. This problem can be solved only when economic conditions in other European countries become normal, which is a question of time. The Labour Government, however, had a great success in reconciling Germany and France on the question of the payment of reparation money. The French Government complained that German industry grew more active than ever and her taxation of the people continued to be comparatively light, yet her deliveries of reparation coal and timber were often in arrears. As a penalty for non-payment the French and Belgian forces occupied the Ruhr (1923). The British Government did not believe that the occupation of the

Ruhr was in the interest of Germany and France.

The Dawes Settlement.

Mr. Ramsay Macdonald called a Conference of the Powers in London (August 1924). This Conference decided that the great railway system of Germany should be added over to an international company and its revenues pledged for the payment of reparation. He also tried to come to a better understanding with Russia by recognising the Soviet Government, but in this measure he lost the support of the Liberal Party. Mr. Macdonald appealed to the country, with the result that in the new election Mr. Baldwin came to power in November 1924. This time he had a large majority over the other two parties.

Affairs in Ireland.

Even after the suppression of the Easter Rebellion (1916) the activities of the Sinn Fein party remained unabated. A new Home Rule Bill (1920) failed to make things better. A Peace Conference in London resulted in a treaty, according to which Southern Ireland was formed into a self-governing Free State within the Commonwealth of Nations. This arrangement solved a thorny problem which had so long baffled solution. The extreme party under De Valera continued to give trouble for some time, but the Irish election of 1923 seemed to prove that the Irish Free State was well established. The followers of De Valera have now decided to take the oath of allegiance and sit in the Dail.*

**Note.*—The Irish name for their Parliament.

The Northern States continue to send their representatives to the British Parliament.

Egypt. In Egypt there was a great political unrest after the War. In 1922, the Government of Mr. Lloyd George recognised the independence of Egypt. England still has certain special rights in that country, especially the right of keeping troops in the zone of the Suez Canal.

Conclusion. The story of the Great War has a warning and a lesson. Little did the dastardly assassin who shot the Archduke know that his shot would be a signal for the greatest tragedy of the world. It humbled to the dust the ambition of powerful rulers, and new nations and institutions sprang up on the ruins of the past. The sanctity of the pledged word was once again established, and humanity saw that though might might rule for some time, right prevailed in the end.

It will take the world much time to recover from the terrible shock of the war. Each nation is now faced with its own domestic issues of vital importance. In Britain there is the Labour question with the possible danger of the clash of classes, and India is torn with communal discord and disunion. The Bolshevik cloud threatens to loom large on the horizon. The problems of peace are no less difficult than those of war.

The foregoing pages have shown how Britain, by slow and steady progress on Constitutional lines, solved her religious and political controversies in the past and rose to be one of the greatest Powers the world has ever known.

History, they say, is a wise and true guide. And the lesson of history to India is clear. The Indians need the same spirit of service and sacrifice, of co-operation and comradeship, of labour and work, of patience and perseverance that won the Great War. 'Peace hath her victories no less renowned than War.'